THE MARRIAGE YOU'VE ALWAYS WANTED

GARY CHAPMAN

#1 *New York Times* Bestselling Author of
THE 5 LOVE LANGUAGES

THE MARRIAGE YOU'VE ALWAYS WANTED

MOODY PUBLISHERS
CHICAGO

Edited by Elizabeth Cody Newenhuyse
Cover design: Mark Arnold
Interior design: Erik M. Peterson
Creative direction: Propeller
Author photo: P.S. Photography

Library of Congress Cataloging in Publication Data

Chapman, Gary D.
    the marriage you've always wanted / Gary Chapman
        p. cm.
    Includes bibliographical references.
    ISBN13: 978-0-8024-1157-0
        1. Marriage—Religious aspects—Christianity. I. Title.
    BV835.C457 2005
    248.8'44—dc22

                                                    2005007219

We hope you enjoy this book from Moody Publishers. Our goal is to provide high-quality, thought-provoking books and products that connect truth to your real needs and challenges. For more information on other books and products written and produced from a biblical perspective, go to www.moodypublishers.com or write to:

Moody Publishers
820 N. LaSalle Boulevard
Chicago, IL 60610

7 9 10 8 6

Printed in the United States of America

Dedicated to
Karolyn

OTHER BOOKS BY GARY CHAPMAN

CONTENTS

ACKNOWLEDGMENTS

I AM INDEBTED to the many couples who have allowed me to enter into the privacy of their lives and probe for better understanding and more effective ways of relating. In private sessions and in small group meetings, many have heard the ideas presented here and have come back with practical suggestions, many of which have been worked into the fabric of this volume. I have used their stories but changed their names to protect their privacy.

I am grateful to Tricia Kube, my administrative assistant, for help not only in preparing much of the manuscript but for completing office tasks, which allowed me time to think and write. Betsey Newenhuyse of Moody Publishers deserves a great deal of credit for sifting through the original text, keeping the best, and requesting of me new material where needed. She has done an excellent job of blending the original and the new.

It would be unfair not to mention those who so many years ago helped me with the original text, *Toward a Growing Marriage*: Melinda Powell, Ellie Shaw, Karen Dresser, Doris Manuel, and my wife, Karolyn. They all worked without pay to help put together the thoughts of a young counselor into what became a helpful tool for thousands of couples. For all of them, I am deeply grateful.

The editorial and administrative teams at Moody Publishers have done an excellent job in formatting, packaging, and producing this book. I view them as my extended family.

INTRODUCTION

THE STATISTICS ARE SOBERING.

According to Christian researcher George Barna, 35 percent of what he calls "born again" Christians—those who have accepted Jesus Christ as Savior and Lord—have experienced a divorce. Worse, 23 percent—nearly a quarter—have been divorced more than once! "But," you say, "surely Christians divorce less than nonbelievers." Not so, says Barna: the figures are identical. Thirty-five percent for "us," 35 percent for "them."[1]

And, from the boomers on down, the younger generations are much more likely to divorce than were their elders. Some estimate that half of all couples marrying today will someday split up. And thousands of other couples who love and follow Jesus are living together in something far less than the "abundant life" that He promised.

Clearly, being Christian and "in love" is not enough for a successful marriage. In my years of counseling, I have seen many couples go from "Everything is perfect!" to "I can't stand him (or her)." How can a couple's hopes plummet from the heights of Mount Everest to the depths of the ocean bottom, often in a matter of months?

It's an old lesson, but a lesson every generation needs to relearn: marital happiness is not automatic.

Fortunately, God has not left us without help. In the Bible, He tells us how to live. In Jesus, He showed us how to live. And husbands and wives, no matter if they are newlyweds or grizzled marital veterans, can learn and grow from this wisdom. It is profound and time-tested. The thousands of couples I speak to, counsel, and hear from attest to the value of these biblically based insights. Put simply, they work.

Of course, mere intellectual exposure to the truth bears little fruit. It is the practical application of that truth that produces fruit. In other words, don't just read this, nod, and say, "Dr. Chapman, you're right!" I would urge both of you, wife and husband, to complete the suggested "Your Turn" reflections at the end of each chapter. As you read, reflect on, and discuss the ideas presented here, do so prayerfully and hopefully, committing your marriage anew to the God who created marriage—and who cares about your marriage in particular.

GARY CHAPMAN, PHD

CHAPTER ONE

Why Do People Marry?

BEFORE WE LAUNCH into a discussion of *how* to make a marriage work, perhaps we ought to pause long enough to ask, "What is the purpose of marriage?" What are we trying to accomplish in marriage?

If you asked a dozen friends those two questions and asked them to write their answers privately, how many different answers do you think you would receive? Here are some of the responses I've received from both singles and marrieds:

- Sex
- Companionship
- Love
- To provide a home for children
- Social acceptance
- Economic advantage
- Security

Current national debates over the meaning of marriage have pushed these questions to the forefront. Some proclaim, "But you can have all these things without marriage!" You don't have to be married to have sexual relations—our society decided that one decades ago. In an era when half of all households are occupied by singles, according to the latest census, being married no longer guarantees social acceptance or economic advantage. Cohabiting is on the rise. What of love, security, companionship, and a home for children? Can these not be accomplished to some degree without marriage? Then why marriage?

To fully respond to these questions, we need to look through the eyes of faith, seeking God's wisdom. And in the Bible, we see a much different picture. Beginning with Genesis, the first book of the Bible where we read the creation story, we find that God's idea of marriage is the blending of two lives in the deepest possible way into a new unit that will both satisfy the individuals involved and serve the purposes of God in the highest possible manner.

COMPANIONSHIP AND COMMITMENT

The heart of humankind cries out for companionship. We are social creatures. God Himself said of Adam, "It is not good for the man to be alone" (Genesis 2:18). I would remind you that this analysis was before the fall of humanity, and that this man already had the warm, personal fellowship of God. Yet God said, "That is not enough!"

God's answer to man's need was to create woman (Genesis 2:18). The Hebrew word used here is one that literally means "face-to-face." That is, God created one with whom the man could have a face-to-face relationship. It speaks of that kind of in-depth personal relationship whereby the two are united in an unbreakable union that satisfies the deepest longings of the human heart. Marriage was God's answer for humankind's deepest human need—union of life with another.

This unity is to encompass all of life. It is not simply a physical relationship. Nor is it simply the giving and receiving of emotional support. It is rather the total union of two lives on the intellectual, social, spiritual, emotional, and physical levels.

This kind of union cannot come without the deep and enduring *commitment* that God intends to accompany marriage. Marriage is not a contract to make sexual relationships acceptable. It is not merely a social institution to provide for the care of children. It is more than a psychological clinic where we gain the emotional support we need. It is more than a means for gaining social status or economic security. The ultimate purpose of marriage is not even achieved when it is a vehicle for love and companionship, as valuable as these are.

> *The supreme purpose of marriage is the union of two individuals at the deepest possible level and in all areas.*

The supreme purpose of marriage is the union of two individuals at the deepest possible level and in all areas, which in turn brings the greatest possible sense of fulfillment to the couple and at the same time serves best the purposes of God for their lives.

WHAT DOES IT MEAN TO BE "ONE"?

Obviously, simply getting married does not guarantee unity. There is a difference between "being united" and "unity." As the old country preacher used to say, "When you tie the tails of two cats together and hang them across the fence, you have united them, but then unity is a different matter."

Perhaps the best biblical example that we have of this kind of unity is God Himself. It is interesting that the word used for "one" in Genesis 2:24, where God says, "This explains why a man leaves his father and mother and is joined to his wife, and the two are united into *one*" (italics added), is the same Hebrew word used of God Himself in Deuteronomy 6:4 where we read, "Hear, O Israel: The Lord our God, the Lord is *one*" (NIV, italics added).

The word "one" speaks of composite unity as opposed to absolute unity. The Scriptures reveal God to be Father, Son, and Spirit, yet one. We do not have three Gods but one God, triune in nature. Illustrations of the Trinity are many, and all break down at some point, but let me use a very common one to illustrate some of the implications of this unity.

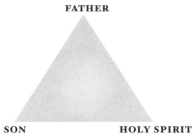

The triangle may be placed on any side, and the *Father*, *Son*, and *Spirit* labels may be moved to any position. It makes no difference, for God is one. What we cannot do is erase one side or remove one title. It must all stand together. God is triune, and God is one. We cannot fully understand this statement, yet we must speak of God in this manner, because this is the manner in which He has revealed Himself. We would not know that God is triune unless God had revealed Himself as triune. We would not know that the Trinity is a unity except that God has revealed it as such.

God is *unity*. On the other hand, God is *diversity*. We cannot rightly say that there are no distinctions among the Trinity. Strictly speaking, the Holy Spirit did not die for us upon the cross. That was the work of the Son. As believers, we are not indwelt by the Father but by the Spirit. The members of the Trinity do have varying roles, yet unity. It is unthinkable that members of the Trinity would ever operate as separate entities. From Genesis 1:26 where God said, "Let *us* make human beings in *our* image" (italics added) to Revelation 22:16–21, we find the Trinity working together as a composite unity.

What implications does this divine unity have for marriage? Here is a second triangle:

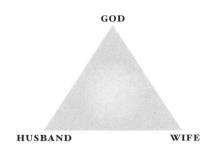

This time the triangle may not be tilted to rest on another side. God must remain at the apex of a Christian marriage. We can, however, exchange the labels *husband* and *wife*, for they are to be one.

In our individualistic age, "unity" is not a prized concept. Yet marital unity is not the kind of unity that eradicates personality. Rather, it is the kind of unity that frees you to express your own diversity, yet experience complete oneness with your mate. You are free to be all that God intends you to be, while experiencing all that God intended when He united us in marriage. No truth could be more liberating and satisfying.

Whether you are just beginning your new life as husband and wife, or are marital veterans working your way through some challenges, I hope that you have clearly in mind the goal of marriage—unity on the deepest possible level in all areas of life. Maybe that is only a dream for you, but if you are willing to work at it, it can become reality. Can you imagine what it would be like to have a degree of intellectual oneness? Social oneness? Spiritual oneness? Physical oneness? Do not give up. You may be on the brink of a new discovery.

"But my spouse is not interested in working with me," you say. "I can't do it all by myself." True, but you can do *something* by yourself. And that something just may be used of God to stimulate change in your mate. I believe that the principle discussed in the following chapter is the number one principle for marital happiness and good health. Read carefully, think clearly, and do not forget the assignment at the end of each chapter.

Your Turn

1. *Take a good look at your marriage. We must recognize weaknesses before we can initiate improvements. On a separate sheet, make four parallel columns with the following headings:*

   Intellectual   **Social**   **Physical**   **Spiritual**

   Under each of these headings, list the characteristics you feel you hold in common with your mate. In which area is your oneness weakest? What could you do to stimulate growth in this area? What will you do?

2. *Suggest that your mate read the chapter, make a similar list, and answer the above questions. When you are both feeling good and open to growth, share your results and agree upon action that will increase your oneness. Concentrate on one area at a time.*

CHAPTER TWO

"Why Won't They Change?"

HEATHER WAS SMILING when she came into my office. But as we were set-tling in and I asked her, "And what is on your mind today?" the smile departed and she started crying.

"I don't know," she said. "There are so many things. Sometimes I feel over-whelmed. It's my marriage. Tyler and I can't seem to understand each other. We spend a lot of time arguing. Some days I feel like giving up."

"What are the issues over which you argue?" I asked.

"Lots of things," she said. "I just don't feel that Tyler is willing to meet me halfway. He doesn't help with the baby much and does almost nothing around the house. He says that his new job takes all of his energy, but I'm tired too. On Saturday, he says he needs to recuperate from the week. Well, maybe I'd like to relax too, but I can't. Somebody has to take care of things. If he would help me, then maybe we both could have some free time."

Two weeks later I was able to talk with Tyler. I asked the question, "How would you describe the problems in your relationship with Heather?"

"She's so demanding," he said. "I can't ever do enough for her. If I go buy groceries, she complains because I forgot the baby shampoo. All she does is complain, so I've almost quit trying.

"Besides all of that," he said, "we have almost no intimacy."

"You mean sex?" I inquired.

"Yes," he said. "Since Emma was born it's gone way down. I don't think that's what marriage ought to be, but I can't seem to get her to understand that."

Heather and Tyler have serious problems in their relationship. But each describes the problem in terms of their mate's behavior. They each believe that if the other would change, they could have a good marriage.

The two are essentially saying the same thing. "My problem is my husband/wife. I am basically a nice person, but my partner has made me miserable."

The pattern is always the same. We pour out our feelings against our mates, describing our problems in terms of our mate's failures.

My spouse does not change, and therefore I am destined to misery. Do not believe it!

When I counsel couples, I often give them paper and pencil and ask them to write for me the things they dislike about their partner. You should see the lists. Some have to request additional paper. They write furiously and freely. Then, a bit later, I ask that they list for me what they feel to be their own weaknesses. Their response is amusing. Usually they can think of one weakness right away, so they write that one down. Then they have to really think to come up with that second one. Some never find it. Is that not amazing? Only one little thing wrong with me (or at most three or four), but my mate has dozens of failures.

FINDING FAULT—IN YOURSELF

If my spouse would just get straightened out, we could have a happy marriage, we reason. So we nag, we fuss, we demand, we cry, we withdraw, we despair—all to no avail.

My spouse does not change, and therefore I am destined to misery. Do not believe it! *Your marriage can improve and improvement can begin today, regardless of your partner's attitude.*

There is a strategy for improvement, spoken by Jesus and recorded in Matthew 7:1–5. In the following quotation, I am substituting "partner" for the word "friend" so that we may see the principle at work in marriage.

> Do not judge others, and you will not be judged. For you will be treated as you treat others. The standard you use in judging is the standard by which you will be judged. And why worry about a speck in your partner's eye when you have a log in your own? How can you think of saying to your partner, "Let me help you get rid of that speck in your eye," when you can't see past the log in your own eye? Hypocrite! First get rid of the log in your own eye; then you will see well enough to deal with the speck in your partner's eye.

Now, please do not misunderstand. I am not calling anyone a hypocrite. I am simply quoting a principle taught by Jesus. Jesus is saying that if one tries to improve her marriage by getting her husband to change (working hard to get the speck out of his eye), energies are being expended in the wrong direction. The place to begin is with one's own failures (the plank or beam in one's own eye).

I am not suggesting that the partner does not have weaknesses or faults. What I am saying is that trying to deal with the faults of the partner is not the place to begin. The first question for any of us when we are in a marital storm is, "What's wrong with *me*? What are my faults?"

This approach may seem strange to you, for after all, your partner is 95 percent of the problem. Right? You are not perfect, but your failure is only minimal. Certainly not more than 5 percent. Let us assume that this is true, though the percentages may change as you begin reflection. Even if you are only 5 percent of the problem, the key to improvement lies with you. Jesus said, "First get rid of the log in your own eye."

What are the mechanics for doing this? How do you go about extracting a "log" from your eye? I suggest that you get alone with God, preferably in a place where you can talk aloud. (If you really feel strong hostility toward your mate, you may want to make a written list of his or her faults beforehand. This may help free the mind psychologically, so that you can deal with your own failures.)

MAKING A LIST

Now, alone with God, simply ask, "Lord, what's wrong with *me*? What are my faults? What are my sins? I know that my mate has many, and I have already written those down, but right now what I want to know is: What are my sins?" Get your pencil and paper (or tablet) ready, for that is a prayer God will answer. Make a list of your sins.

You may find the sin of bitterness, which is condemned in Ephesians 4:31: "Get rid of all bitterness, rage, anger, harsh words, and slander, as well as all types of evil behavior." Certainly your partner may have triggered your negative attitude, but you are the one who allowed bitterness to develop. It is always wrong to be bitter toward one of God's creatures.

You may find the sin of unkindness, which is in violation of the command of Ephesians 4:32: "Be kind to each another, tenderhearted, forgiving one another, just as God through Christ has forgiven you."

"But my mate has not done anything to deserve my kindness!" you protest. True, but *you* are the one who decides to be kind or unkind. Absence of kindness is always wrong for the Christian.

You may discover lack of love toward your mate. We will discuss this further in chapter 3, but let me say here that love as described in 1 Corinthians 13 is an act or attitude more than an emotion. "Love is patient and kind . . . not jealous or boastful or proud or rude. It does not demand its own way. It is not irritable, and it keeps no record of being wronged" (vv. 4–5). When you fail to express love to your partner, you have sinned.

The Holy Spirit may bring many sins to your mind. Write them down one by one until you can think of no other, then open your Bible and read 1 John 1:9 (NIV): "If we confess our sins, he is faithful and just and will forgive us our sins and purify us from all unrighteousness." In making your list you have really confessed your sin, for you have agreed with God that these things are wrong in your life.

ACCEPTING GOD'S FORGIVENESS

I suggest, however, that you go back over the list and agree again with God that these are wrong and, at the same time, thank Him for Christ's death on the cross and therefore for forgiveness. In your own words you are saying, "Father, this is wrong—so wrong. How could I be so foolish? But I want to thank You for the cross—that Christ has paid for this sin, and I can be forgiven. Thank You, Father, for forgiveness."

Work through your list and accept God's forgiveness for every past failure. God does not intend us to live under the emotional load of past failures. We can be forgiven.

A CLEAR CONSCIENCE

After the acceptance of God's forgiveness, there is a second step toward a growing, God-honoring marriage. The apostle Paul states it in Acts 24:16 as a basic principle in his own life: "I always try to maintain a clear conscience before God and all people."

I believe that in this statement we have the most important principle of mental health and, consequently, of marital health. Paul is not saying that he never did anything wrong, but rather that, having done wrong, he has also cleared his conscience, first toward God and then toward people. We empty our conscience toward God when we confess our sins. We empty our conscience toward a spouse when we go to him or her and confess our failures.

"But what if my spouse isn't willing to forgive me?" That is his problem and not yours. Your responsibility is to admit the wrong you carry and ask forgiveness. Your mate's response is not your responsibility. You have done what you can do by dealing with your wrong. You have not done what you can do until you have dealt with your own offenses. You see, you cannot confess your partner's sin, but you can deal with your 5 percent.

You can say to him or her in your own words, after a good meal, "Honey (or whatever title you prefer), God has dealt with me today, and I now realize that I have been wrong in so many things. I have confessed them to God and want to ask your forgiveness. I have been very selfish in demanding that you _____. I have not been very kind in _____. I have failed in meeting your needs for _____. And I want to ask, will you forgive me?" Be as specific with your mate as you have been with God. Give him or her a chance to respond.

What will happen when you do this? It may be the dawning of a new day. On the other hand, your spouse may say, "Oh yeah, I've heard that before, and I don't believe it." What you do at this point will determine whether you must have another confession session with God, or whether you will go on to improve your marriage. If you explode with tears, words, or flying saucers, you will need to retreat to ask God's forgiveness for another failure.

Why not respond by saying, "I can understand your feelings. I know that I have confessed before, and I know that I have failed many times to be what I want to be. So I understand that you find it hard to believe that things will be any different this time."

Do not make rash promises about the future. Right now, you are dealing with the past. Seal your confession with an embrace and a kiss if your spouse is willing. Smile even if you are pushed away.

TEAR DOWN THIS WALL!

Do not worry about your spouse's response to your confession. Do not think he should fall on his knees and confess his own wrong. He may, and if so, great! You will have a tender evening. But negative feelings may not capitulate that easily. Personal pride stands as a hurdle for all of us. Allow time for God's work in your mate. When you have confessed your wrong and emptied your conscience toward God and your partner, you have done the greatest thing you can do for your mate. He may not respond in like manner, but you have made it easier for him to admit wrong.

We cannot manipulate people. Every person has a free will. We can choose to be hateful, cutting, and mean, even in the face of confession. But your marriage will be better *even if your mate never confesses his wrong*, because now you are free to move out to be a positive stimulus for good in the relationship. You are now free to be a part of the solution instead of a part of the problem.

Many couples are at a stalemate because they have allowed a wall to develop between them. Walls are always erected a block at a time. One partner fails in a particular matter. It may be as small a matter as failing to carry out the garbage or as large as failing to meet sexual needs. Instead of dealing with that failure, we ignore it. We excuse ourselves, thinking, "After all, what does she expect? I'm doing my part! Why doesn't she think of *my* needs?"

For whatever reason, one failure after another is ignored until a long, high, thick wall develops between two people who started out "in love." Communication grinds to a halt, and only resentment remains.

How is such a wall to be destroyed? By tearing down those blocks of failure, one by one. As we admit our failure as specifically as possible, we destroy the barrier to growth. Granted, the walls must be torn down from both sides if the relationship is to be ideal, but if you will tear down your side, you make it easier for your spouse to begin demolition. If both are willing to tear down the wall of separation, you can build on the rubble a beautiful relationship.

Once the wall is destroyed by confession and forgiveness, we must practice immediate confession of subsequent failures. We must never allow the wall to be erected again. Confession must become a way of life.

A SMALL WALL GOES UP . . .

Mornings are a frenzied time in a lot of households—a time when tempers can flare. My wife, Karolyn, and I had such a morning once. We were trying to get the kids off to school and me to work, and I said to my wife, "Karolyn, where is my briefcase?"

To which she replied, "I don't know."

I repeated with greater volume, "Come on, Karolyn, I'm in a hurry. Where is my briefcase? I put it right in there by the dresser last night, and it's gone. Where did you put it?"

"Gary, I don't know where your briefcase is!"

We went about two more rounds of this—same message, higher volume. By this time, I was really upset. Obviously she had moved my briefcase, but she was not concerned enough to even think about where she had put it. In anger, I rushed the children out the door and sped them off to school. I talked to them kindly about their schoolwork, but after I let them out, I returned to the business of being furious with Karolyn for misplacing my briefcase.

I went the entire nine miles from my children's school to my office fuming, "How could I have married such a scatterbrain? My briefcase is important. In fact, I can't operate without it. What am I going to do today?"

That question was answered the moment I walked into my office. There sat my briefcase, right where I had left it the day before.

At that point, I had several choices. I could dismiss the matter, promise myself that I would never let Karolyn know where I had found my briefcase, and hope that she would never ask. I could rationalize that my response to her was because of fatigue, distraction, lack of exercise—any excuse would do. Or I could practice what I preach, that is, behold the plank, confess my sin, and ask forgiveness.

A WALL COMES DOWN

So I turned to God and said, "O God, how could I be so foolish? Forgive me for the horrible way in which I treated Karolyn—for the lack of love, the unkind, critical, accusing words, the bitter spirit. Thank You, Father, for the cross. Thank You that the penalty has been paid. Thank You for forgiveness." My conscience was emptied toward God.

Next was the phone call. "Karolyn, I . . . uh . . . I . . . uh . . . found my brief-case."

"Yes," she said.

"It was here at the office," I haltingly continued. "I'm really sorry about the way I talked to you. It was horrible, and it was wrong, and I want to ask, Will you forgive me?"

Do you know what she said? "I thought you'd call!"

She knew I would call because we have committed ourselves to keeping the wall from growing thick and high. She knew that I would not go long with that failure unresolved. Life is too short to let high, heavy walls develop. Why waste life? A wall will never stand if you deal with each failure as it occurs.

Perhaps you are thinking, "Raising one's voice over a briefcase is a little failure. My failures are in a whole different category." I remember the husband who said to me after hearing my lecture, "Getting the Beam Out of Your Own Eye," "I never thought this could happen to me. My wife and I have a fairly good marriage. We've always prided ourselves on being committed to each other. But six months ago, a lady started working for our company who triggered something inside of me I had not felt for a long time. To be honest with you, it was exciting."

"I KNEW IT HAD GONE TOO FAR"

Jared continued, "We started having lunches together and found it so easy to talk to each other. It was almost like we had known each other for a lifetime. I knew that I should not be feeding this relationship, but I found it so satisfying. She was also married, and one day I got a phone call from her husband, who said that he knew about my relationship with his wife and that if I did not break it off immediately, he would call my wife and expose the whole thing. I was terrified. I spent the afternoon thinking about what would happen to my marriage and my children. Even though we were not sexually involved with each other, I knew that our relationship had gone too far."

Jared was equally concerned about the wall that was building between his wife and himself. She did not know about the relationship, but after tension developed, Jared recognized that "my 'secret' had definitely become an emotional barrier between me and my wife." He had been more aware of the things she did that annoyed him. Later he admitted to me that for several months "I had courted the idea that perhaps life would be better with someone else. I knew that Satan had been leading me down a road that would dishonor Christ.

"On the way home that afternoon, I stopped by a local park and poured out my heart to God in confession for my wrongdoing. I don't remember when I have ever cried so much. I knew that God was willing to forgive me, but I found it so hard to believe that I had allowed Satan to take me this far down the wrong road."

There was more Jared needed to do, of course. That night at home he confessed everything to his wife. He told her he indeed loved her and how sorry he was for permitting himself to have lunch with another woman. He intended to break off the relationship the next day "no matter what," he said.

"I hoped that she would be able to forgive me and that we could continue to rebuild our marriage. She cried and I cried. I guess it had been a long time since either of us had felt so much pain. She said that she wanted to forgive me but she needed some time to sort out her emotions."

The next day he asked the other woman to come to his office, where he said his time with her and responses were wrong. He took full responsibility "for allowing myself to do something that I knew was moving in the wrong direction. I asked her to forgive me for my inappropriate actions and I told her that I hoped she and her husband could work out their marriage."

Jared told her that he wanted to call her husband and apologize to him. "She gave me his phone number and as soon as she left my office, I called him and apologized for being out of line. I assured him that there had been no sexual involvement but I did know that our spending so much time together was wrong. I told him that I had confessed to my wife what had gone on and had asked her to forgive me and that I hoped that she was going to give me a chance to work on our marriage and that I wished the same for him and his wife."

The next night Jared and his wife talked again. They cried once more, and she told him that she was willing to forgive him and that she wanted to work on their marriage. "She asked me if I would be willing to go for counseling, and I willingly agreed. Over the next three months we saw a counselor once a week and worked through not only the pain of my present failure but some of the things we had failed to deal with in the past. All of this happened five years ago, and today we have a wonderful marriage. I am grateful to God that He used an angry husband to wake me up, and I am grateful to my wife for forgiving me."

Repentance makes possible the reality of forgiveness, and what forgiveness brings.

Jared's story demonstrates three realities: (1) sin is deceiving; (2) God cares for His erring children; and (3) repentance is always the better choice. Repentance makes possible the reality of forgiveness, and what forgiveness brings.

NOT BY OURSELVES

Of course, we cannot do this on our own. Humanly, this is beyond any of us. A third step must accompany the first two: yielding to the ministry of the Holy Spirit.

This isn't always an easy concept for us to understand. But Jesus left us with a promise and a description. In John 14, speaking to His twelve disciples during the Last Supper—and knowing their fear and impending feelings of aloneness when their Master's earthly ministry was ended—Jesus promised to send a "Comforter" who would lead them into all truth. Paul tells us that the Spirit indwells every believer (Romans 8:9). It is the Holy Spirit who rebukes us when we are wrong (Hebrews 12:5) and motivates confession; it is the Holy Spirit whose task it is to produce in us the qualities and characteristics seen in the life of Jesus and called the "fruit of the Spirit"—love, joy, peace, patience, kindness, goodness, faithfulness, gentleness, and self-control (Galatians 5:22–23 NIV).

Notice that these characteristics are called the "fruit of the Spirit" rather than the fruit of self-effort. The Christian life is not a commitment to *try* to be like Jesus. Rather, it is *yielding* our lives to the Holy Spirit so that He can express the qualities of Jesus through us.

YIELDING TO SOMEONE GREATER THAN OURSELVES

We cannot work hard enough to produce peace. Peace comes as a by-product of yielding our lives fully to the Holy Spirit. The same is true of joy, patience, gentleness, goodness, and all the other qualities listed above. The key to the Christian's victory is recognizing and accepting the control of the Holy Spirit.

How then are we filled with the Holy Spirit, or controlled by the Holy Spirit? Having confessed our sins and accepted God's forgiveness, we then ask Him to fill us, or control us, totally by His Spirit. That is, we ask the Holy Spirit to ascend the throne of our lives. That is a prayer God will answer because John says, "We are confident that he hears us whenever we ask for anything that pleases him" (1 John 5:14). We know it "pleases him" to fill us with His Spirit because of the command in Ephesians 5:18: "Be filled with the Holy Spirit." Therefore, when we ask Him to fill us, or control us, we know that He will.

We accept the Spirit's control over our lives by faith. We do not wait nor plead for some great emotional experience. Having confessed our sins and asked for His control, we simply believe that He is working within us, and we journey along through life, trusting that through God's Spirit we can nurture our marriages through candor, confession, and forgiveness.

Briefly, here's how we can yield to the Holy Spirit and enhance our marriages.

1. I realize that my marriage is not what it should be.
2. I stop blaming my mate and ask God to show me where I am at fault.
3. I confess my sin and accept God's forgiveness, according to 1 John 1:9.

4. I ask Him to fill me with His Spirit and give me the power to make constructive changes in my life.

5. In His power, I go to my mate, confess my failures, and ask forgiveness.

6. In His power, I go on to change my behavior, words, and attitudes, according to the principles that I discover in Scripture.

If you do this, be assured that you and your spouse will be closer to building the marriage you've always wanted.

BUT WHAT ABOUT *HIM*?

I do not wish to communicate the idea that you are not to discuss the faults of your mate. Let me give a personal illustration that indicates the role of confession as it relates to discussion of faults.

One summer Saturday years ago, my wife and I were having lunch with our two children, enjoying the beauty of the view outside our window. Birds were singing, flowers blooming, and our hearts were glad—glad until Karolyn made the announcement that she was going to take our son to the shopping center and get him some shoes. Rather soon after the announcement, she left. Dirty dishes were still on the table.

Being a mature person, of course I did not say anything, but as she drove off down the street, I retreated to the back porch, made myself comfortable in my rocker, and proceeded to get angry with her. With the aid of my melancholic personality, I thought all kinds of morose thoughts.

"After all, this is my only day off. I always try to be at home on Saturdays. She doesn't work outside the home. She had every day of the week to go shopping. Why wait until Saturday? Obviously, she doesn't love me or she would not leave me alone. Well, she didn't really leave me alone. There are all those dirty dishes on the table. The least she could have done was to have cleaned up the table. I guess she expects me to do that. Well, I'll show her. I am not her servant."

The thoughts went from bad to worse, and I succeeded in making myself miserable in the presence of singing birds and blooming flowers. Then there came to my mind very quietly—almost as though God hesitated to disturb my misery—the title of my lecture "Behold the Beam" and Jesus' words "First get rid of the log in your own eye."

Turning to God, I said, "O Lord, how foolish! How stupid! What's wrong with me that I can get so upset over my wife going to the shopping center?" The answer came quickly. First, I was judging my wife's motives for her decision, saying that she left because she did not love me or think of me. Such judging is condemned by Jesus in Matthew 7:1. (Incidentally, such judging is also foolish, for no one can know the motives of another unless that person chooses to reveal them.) Second, my attitude was very selfish. Having confessed these and accepted God's forgiveness, I yielded the throne of my life to the Holy Spirit and was able to wash the dishes with an optimistic spirit and a positive attitude toward my wife.

That evening, after the children were in bed, I had a chance to relate to my wife my afternoon problem. "You know, Babe," I said, "I had a real struggle this afternoon. So much of a struggle, in fact, that I sinned and God had to deal with me about it. Now, I've confessed it, and God has forgiven me, but I thought you might like to know about it."

How could she resist? I proceeded to tell her about my attitudes and thoughts, and that I had seen how wrong they were. I did not need to confess to her, because she had not even seen me at my point of failure. My confession had been to God, but I told her because our goal is oneness—as we saw in the previous chapter. Oneness is attained only as we are willing to confide failures as well as successes. When I disclosed my problem and my confession to God, my wife was very open to discussing the episode, and we agreed upon some guidelines for the future that were mutually acceptable. You see, my confession had paved the way for a constructive conversation about her action.

It should be noted here that Karolyn had done nothing morally wrong. Shopping on Saturday is not a sin. I was the one who had sinned. When I acknowledged my problem, rather than pointing an accusing finger at her, she was free emotionally to discuss her action and ask, "What can I do to help with this problem?"

How different the results would have been had I decided to continue in my misery and allowed bitterness to grow! When she came home, I could have laid into her with condemnation or sulked in silence and let her beg me to reveal the reason for my animosity. I could have buried my feelings, not dealing with them, letting them smolder underneath the surface. None of those responses would have been helpful to our marriage.

Whenever a relationship breaks down, both people are a part of the breakdown. One may bear more of the responsibility than the other, but either can move to restore it. They must each deal with the wrong they personally bear, and, indeed, that is all either party can do. Confession is a personal act. We must allow each other the freedom to decide whether or not to confess. In the meantime, we can confess our failure, and this may be the stimulus that triggers confession on the part of our mate.

In this chapter, we have discussed a way to turn your marriage around and put it on the road toward health. After the first major confession, you will not need to make a list of your faults, but you should deal with them one by one as they occur. On any given day when you become aware of friction, ill feelings, and lack of oneness in your relationship, the first question should be "Lord, what's wrong with me? Why should I be so upset over that? What did I do or fail to do that may have stimulated that action from my mate? Even if she is totally wrong in her action, what about my attitude? Is my response to that action right or wrong?"

As you see where you are wrong, confess it, accept God's forgiveness, and ask His Spirit to control you. People do not "make us miserable." We choose to be miserable. The immediate emotion that arises after the action of your partner may be automatic and beyond your control, but what you *do* with that emotion is your decision.

If you are willing to search your own heart and confess any wrong discovered, then you can feel at peace, even though you are not particularly happy with the situation at hand. You then can be a positive force for change, rather than compounding the problem with your attitude.

IN CLOSING

It's important to remember that your marriage can be improved even if your partner never changes. One partner can change a marriage for the better even when the other has no desire for improvement. I am not saying that you can have an ideal marriage, fully satisfying in every area. That, indeed, takes the work of two individuals under God. But you can see substantial growth in your marriage, if only you are willing to change.

If you will take the kind of action suggested in this chapter, you will be taking the first and most strategic steps toward a healthy, growing marriage. Who knows what God will do with your mate if you serve as a helper instead of a hinderer?

Your Turn

1. *Make a list of your spouse's weaknesses. Where is he/she failing? (We will talk later about how to use this list. For the present, simply make the list so that you can free your mind to look at your own needs.)*

2. *Read in your Bible the following: Matthew 7:1–5; Acts 24:16; 1 John 1:9.*

3. *Make a list of your own sins and confess them to God in the manner described in this chapter.*

4. *Ask for, and accept by faith, the control of the Holy Spirit over your life.*

5. *As a person forgiven by God and controlled by the Spirit, disclose your failures to your mate and ask his/her forgiveness.*

6. *Whenever you have a wrong attitude or action, judge it immediately and experience forgiveness. Discipline yourself to live with a clear conscience toward God and your mate.*

7. *Life is too short to be at odds with anyone. You deserve the liberty of a clear conscience. Confession of wrong and asking for forgiveness is the road to freedom. Why wait?*

CHAPTER THREE

What Love Really Means

WHAT DOES IT MEAN to really love your spouse? Perhaps not what you think.

If you took a survey among your married friends (guaranteeing anonymity) and asked them to rate themselves on a scale of 1 to 10, with 1 being "total commitment to my own self-interest" and 10 signifying "total commitment to my mate's welfare," I predict most would fall around 5. Because if we are honest, most of us are thinking about what we are going to get out of the relationship—how wonderful it is going to be for us.

Is that love? For the past several years I have asked various seminar study groups to give me their definitions of love. Definitions have varied greatly. Some have placed a strong emphasis upon the emotional-physical aspect of love, whereas others have emphasized the self-giving nature of love. One I like is: "Love is a four-letter word composed of two consonants, L and V; two vowels, O and E; and two fools, you and me."

Without trying to define love further at this point, I want to share two very strange statements in Scripture. In Ephesians 5:25, husbands are admonished, "Love your wives," and in Titus 2:3–4, the older women are advised, "Train the younger women to love their husbands." I would remind you that the grammatical construction in Ephesians 5:25 is the same as that in verse 18 (NIV), where we read, "Be filled with the Spirit." It is a command.

Could it be that what we have called "love" is not love at all?

Why would a man have to be commanded to love his wife, and a woman have to be taught to love her husband? Is that not what marriage is all about? Is this not why you got married in the first place? That is what most couples tell me when they come to discuss marriage. Why, then, after marriage do we have to be commanded to love?

Could it be that what we have called "love" is not love at all? Could it be that for most couples, love comes after the wedding, if indeed it is ever realized?

THE BEST DESCRIPTION OF LOVE EVER

Let us look at 1 Corinthians 13:4–8 for the best description (not definition) of love that I have ever found. Read it slowly, with thought as to what implications it would have in marriage. The passage is often read at weddings, inspiring even unbelievers with its beauty and poetry. Few, however, see its practical implications.

"Love is patient and kind. Love is not jealous or boastful or proud or rude. It does not demand its own way. It is not irritable, and it keeps no record of being wronged. It does not rejoice about injustice but rejoices whenever the truth wins out. Love never gives up, never loses faith, is always hopeful, and endures through every circumstance."

The passage is too strong to digest at one sitting, so just take a few of the key ideas. Love is patient and kind, never demanding its own way; not a "know-it-all" but understanding, slow to take offense; courteous; it exhibits a positive attitude toward problems. All these characteristics of love are directed toward the well-being of the one loved.

But do these qualities of love require a warm "feeling" toward the one loved? Do not answer too hurriedly. How warm do you have to feel to be kind—to be patient? You see, the kind of love described in 1 Corinthians 13 does not emphasize emotion but attitude and action—which are not beyond our control.

"I DON'T LOVE HER ANYMORE"

Often couples come to me in the midst of marriage difficulty. They are at the point of separating, and when I ask why, they make known their points of contention and conclude with the clincher, "Well, we just don't love each other anymore." That is supposed to settle it. Divorce is the only alternative. After all, we cannot help it. We have simply "lost our love." Or "It's beyond our control." One husband said, "I wish I could love her, but it's too late. Too much has happened."

I do not believe that. If you want sympathy with that view, do not come to see me. I would do you a great disservice if I led you to believe that your marital happiness is "beyond your control."

Let me give you the second half of the sentence I pointed out earlier. In Ephesians 5:25 we read, "For husbands, this means love your wives, just as Christ loved the church. He gave up his life for her." Well, what was the attitude of the church when Christ gave Himself for it? Were those whom He loved kind, considerate, and patient toward Him? On the contrary, the best among them cursed and said, "I don't know the man!" (Matthew 26:74). Romans 5:8 states that God showed His love toward us in that while we were filthy, selfish, and hateful, Christ died for us.

God loved us when we were very unlovely. So a husband is commanded to love his wife even when she isn't very lovable. You see, any man can love a woman who loves him. You do not need to be commanded to do that. That is the kind of love we knew before we got married. I was lovely to her because she was lovely to me, but how am I to respond now that my partner is not lovely? This is where the biblical admonition gives us help. If I respond with kindness, understanding, patience, and courtesy, I am making it as easy as possible for her to respond in like manner.

Now this does not mean that she must respond with love. She has the freedom not to love. That is why the ultimate success of a marriage cannot be achieved by the acts of one partner only. It takes two loving individuals to attain ultimate satisfaction in a relationship. But if I, as one individual, choose to love, things will improve. I can always improve my marriage, and love is my greatest weapon.

RISING ABOVE YOURSELF

I would be unfair if I did not express clearly my deep doubts that you will ever be able to demonstrate such self-giving love without the aid of the Holy Spirit. The Scriptures say, "For we know how dearly God loves us, because he has given us the Holy Spirit to fill our hearts with his love" (Romans 5:5). The ability to respond in love comes from God. I have the opportunity to be God's agent of love to my wife. No one in all the universe is in a better position to love my wife than I. I must not forfeit that opportunity. If I am willing to turn to God, admitting my lack of love, yes, even my bitterness and hatred, and accept His forgiveness and ask Him to love my wife through me, I can become a lover par excellence.

What happens usually is this. My wife does something that I think is wrong or, worse yet, fails to do something that I think she should have done. Immediately, my emotions toward her are negative. These negative emotions may well be spontaneous and beyond my control. But what I do with these emotions is not beyond my control. If I follow my basic nature, I will express those emotions with cutting words or the hurtful silent treatment, either of which will accomplish the job of making both of us miserable. My negative actions will tend to elicit negative reactions from her.

If, however, I choose not to follow my negative emotions, I can be an agent of love. That is, I can thank God that in His power I do not have to be negative just because I feel negative and thus can ask for His ability to express love and turn the whole situation around.

Contrary to some popular psychological notions, all of our negative emotions do not need to be expressed. Some need to be starved.

Let me illustrate. I met Jason in Tucson, Arizona. He was from the East Coast but had moved west two years ago after his marriage ended in divorce. I've never forgotten Jason's graphic description of uncontrolled expression of emotions: "I realize now that I destroyed my own marriage. I allowed my emotions to control my life. Because we were so different, Susan did a lot of things that irritated me. It seemed that almost every day I was telling her that I was hurt, disappointed, frustrated, and angry. It all came across as condemnation to her. I was trying to be open but I realize now that you can't let raw sewage run through a marriage and expect to grow a garden."

Jason's right. We cannot constantly verbalize our negative emotions and expect them to have a positive effect upon our spouse.

I am not suggesting that negative emotions are sinful. Only when I feed my negative emotions with meditation and action do I become guilty of error. The world is filled with couples who have come to the breaking point because they expressed all their negative emotions toward each other. I do not mean that we are to deny that we have such emotions, but rather that we are to express them to God and thank Him that we do not have to follow them.

Some will say, "All right. You are telling me to love my mate regardless of how I feel toward him. Isn't that hypocritical?"

No, there is nothing hypocritical about that unless you are claiming to feel something that you do not feel. When you express kindness by a thoughtful act or a gift, you do not have to claim any warm emotional feeling. You are simply being kind. You may not feel anything, or indeed your feelings may be negative. But it is in the act of expressing love that you are most likely to receive love from your mate, which in turn affects your emotions in a positive manner.

Negative feelings are most often alleviated when they are ignored rather than pampered.

Thousands of marriages could have been redeemed if one partner had discovered the principle of love as we have discussed it. Should you forget everything else taught in this book, remember to love "1 Corinthians 13 style." Love is the greatest of all and is available to all.

Let us assume that you choose to love. Though your feelings may be apathetic or even negative, you choose to be God's channel of love to your mate. How would you express such love? There are two basic ways: by words and by deeds.

LOVING WITH WORDS

In 1 Corinthians 8:1 we read, "Love edifies" (NASB). The word *edify* means "to build up." The noun form is our word *edifice*, or *building*. Therefore, to love my mate means to "build up" my mate. One of the most powerful means of edification is the compliment. Find something small or great that you like about your mate and express appreciation.

The story is told of a woman who went to a marriage counselor for advice. "I want to divorce my husband," she confided, "and I want to hurt him all I can."

"In that case," the counselor advised, "start showering him with compliments. When you have become indispensable to him—when he thinks you love him devotedly—then start the divorce action. That's the way to hurt him most."

Some months later, the wife returned to report that she had followed the suggested course. "Good, now's the time to file for divorce," said the counselor.

"Divorce!" said the woman indignantly. "Never! I've fallen in love with him."

LOVING WITH WORDS WHEN YOU'RE MISTREATED

"But how can I compliment him when he is treating me so horribly?" a wife may ask. By the help of the Holy Spirit, the Bible replies. Is this not the admonition of Jesus when He says in Matthew 5:44, "Love your enemies! Pray for those who persecute you!"? If we love in the face of ill treatment, we may likely redeem our marriage.

If we could learn the tremendous power of the compliment, we would seldom again revert to complaint—as in this example:

The wife looks out the window and observes that her husband has almost completed mowing the front yard. She decides, "This is the time to strike." She goes outside, cups her hands to her mouth, and screams above the noise of the lawn mower, "Do you think you will get around to the gutters this afternoon?" Imagine—her husband has just spent an exhausting two hours mowing the grass, and all she offers is another job assignment. I cannot tell you what he will say, but I can tell you what he will think: "Woman, get off my back!" How much better he would feel if she would come out with a glass of lemonade and tell him how nice the yard looks.

I will not guarantee that your husband will volunteer to clean the gutters, but I will guarantee that the compliment will be received with joy. A husband is far more motivated to attend to household tasks when rewarded by a compliment.

Of course, it works for the husband as well. One wife, married twenty-five years, recalled her irritation when she came home from work, tired, and started fixing dinner. "I was making something with a lot of vegetables. My husband was peering at the pan and saying, 'Where's the meat?' I wanted to bop him and say, 'Fine, *you* cook.'" How much better if the husband could express his appreciation for a good home-cooked meal—even without the meat!

LOVING WITH WORDS OF KINDNESS, ENTREATY, AND ACCEPTANCE

A second way to express love by words is to *speak with kindness.* Love is kind (1 Corinthians 13:4). This has to do with the manner in which you speak. "A gentle answer deflects anger, but harsh words make tempers flare" (Proverbs 15:1). Why do you scream when you talk to your mate? Why do you speak harshly? Because you are following your negative emotions. You can speak kindly even with negative feelings if you choose God's help.

There is nothing wrong with admitting your feelings to your mate if you speak with kindness, particularly when inside you feel like nagging. The wife gently says, "I love you dearly, honey, and you're a great husband—but I need you to look at my laptop like you promised me several weeks ago." It never hurts to throw in a compliment with your kind request.

A third way to speak with love is to use *entreaty* rather than command. Love does not demand its own way (1 Corinthians 13:5). "What do you think of this?" "How about this?" "Is this possible?" "Could we do this?" These are words of entreaty, as opposed to "See that this gets done today!"

Another way to express love is with *words of acceptance*. Assure your mate that he/she can express ideas without your getting defensive and feeling attacked. A wife says, "I feel that you don't really love me like you used to." By nature, the husband responds, "How could you say that? Don't you remember that expensive bag I bought you at the outlet after Christmas and the time I took you out to brunch after church last summer?" What is he doing? He is condemning her for her feelings. How much better to say, "How's that, Babe? What is it that makes you feel that way?" Give her a chance to express her feelings, and then accept her words. Look for ways to minister to those feelings, rather than condemning them.

Speaking with love also means that we use *present-tense words*. Love keeps no record of being wronged, does not dredge up the past with each new crisis. If past failures have been confessed, then why bring them up again? Love speaks only of present facts and does not seek to build a case by referring to every past imperfection. Some couples club each other to death with past failures. This tears down the "edifice" of marriage.

LOVING WITH DEEDS

What would our marriages look like if we truly abided by the counsel of John, "the disciple Jesus loved," to love not with words only but "by our actions" (1 John 3:18)? How do we back up what we say with what we do?

Love is *patient*. Therefore, if we want to express love in our behavior, we must have patient behavior. The implications here are tremendous. This would eliminate your pacing the floor while your wife gets ready to go. Why not sit down and relax? Your impatient behavior does not increase her speed. It simply agitates your own spirit and may even be physically harmful. You do not have to be impatient. You have the choice. Why not love?

Love is *kind*. Acts of kindness are one of love's strongest voices. One is limited only by her imagination and will. Supermarket tulips on a dull winter day say "I love you" to all but the wife who is allergic to flowers. That text message in the midst of the workday to say "You are the greatest husband in the world" may well make it so. A surprise dinner out at a restaurant without a drive-through window communicates "You are special" to a wife who regularly prepares meals for the family.

Do you treat others with more courtesy than you do your mate?

How long has it been since you wrote your mate a love letter? "Don't be silly," someone will say. "I see him every day. Why write a letter?" Because you will say some things in a love letter that you do not say in verbal conversation. A love letter a month will keep a marriage alive and growing. A letter is an act of kindness.

Why not set some new goals for yourself in the area of kindness? Think of something you can do every day to express your love to your mate. Having completed the deed, say verbally, "I love you!" Do not be like the man who told me: "I told my wife I loved her when I asked her to marry me. If I ever change my mind, I'll let her know." Love is not a once-and-for-all act. It is a way of life.

Love is *courteous*. The word *courteous* means "of courtlike manners, polite." Have you forgotten the little things? Do you treat others with more courtesy than you do your mate? Too many of us take the idea of "a man's home is his castle" too far, indulging ourselves in behavior we wouldn't dream of exhibiting in the office or at church. Almost as bad, we overlook the little niceties: simple "good mornings," kisses on coming home from work, taking our wife's arm to guide her over an icy patch in the parking lot. Calling or texting to say "I'll be late" is not more than you would do for anyone else with whom you have an appointment. Why not treat your mate with as much courtesy and respect as you do others?

Love is *unselfish*. Love looks out for the best interest of the person loved. If a husband lived with a view to helping his wife reach her potential, and the wife lived with a view to helping her husband reach his potential, we would be following the biblical ideal.

Perhaps the pattern of love that we have discussed seems supernatural to you. It is! The human norm is to love those who love you. Jesus said, "If you love only those who love you, what reward is there for that? Even corrupt tax collectors do that much" (Matthew 5:46). You do not need God's help to love a husband or wife who loves you. That is natural. But Jesus calls us to "love your enemies!" (Matthew 5:44).

Surely your mate could not be worse than an enemy. Then your responsibility is clear. God wants to express His love through you. Will you give Him a chance to demonstrate the power of love? Let your emotions alone; do not condemn yourself for your negative feelings. In the power of the Holy Spirit, express love in word and in deed, and your emotions will catch up with you. If in time your mate reciprocates your love, the "tingles" may even return. Love is not beyond your grasp if you are a Christian.

IRRITATIONS AND IMPERFECTIONS

If I could paraphrase 1 Peter 4:8—"Love covers a multitude of sins"—I would say, "Love accepts many imperfections." Love does not demand perfection from one's mate. There are some things that your mate either cannot or will not change. These I am calling imperfections. They may not be moral in nature but are simply things that you do not like. May I illustrate from my own marriage?

We had been married several years before I realized that my wife was a "drawer opener," but not a "drawer closer." I do not know if I had been blinded to that fact the first three or four years or if it was a new behavior pattern for her, but at any rate it irritated me greatly.

I did what I thought was the "adult" thing to do. I confronted her with my displeasure in the matter and asked for change. The next week, I observed carefully each time I entered our apartment, but to my dismay there was no change. Each time I saw an open drawer, I fumed. Sometimes I exploded.

After a couple of months, I decided to use my educational expertise. I would give her a visual demonstration along with my lecture. I went home and took everything out of the top bathroom drawer, removed the drawer, and showed her the little wheel on the bottom and how it fit into the track, and explained what a marvelous invention that was. This time, I knew that she understood how the drawer worked and how serious I was about the matter.

The next week, I eagerly anticipated change—but nothing happened! Then one day, I came home to discover that our eighteen-month-old daughter had fallen and cut the corner of her eye on the edge of an open drawer. Karolyn had taken her to the hospital. There she had gone through the ordeal of watching the surgeon stitch up that open wound and wondering if it would leave a scar or impaired vision.

She told me the whole story, and I contained my emotions while I listened. I was proud of myself. I did not even mention the open drawer, but on the inside I was saying, "I bet she'll close those drawers now!" I knew this would be the clincher. She had to change now! But she did not.

After another week or two, the thought crossed my mind, "I don't believe she will ever change!" I sat down to analyze my alternatives. I wrote them down: (1) I could leave her! (2) I could be miserable every time I looked at an open drawer from now until the time I die or she dies, or (3) I could accept her as a "drawer opener" and take on myself the task of closing drawers.

As I analyzed these alternatives, I ruled out number one right away. As I looked at number two, I realized that if I were going to be miserable every time I saw an open drawer from now until I die, I would spend a great deal of my life in misery. I reasoned that the best of my alternatives was number three: Accept this as one of her imperfections.

I made my decision and went home to announce it. "Karolyn," I said, "you know the thing about the drawers?"

"Gary, please don't bring that up again," she replied.

"No, I have the answer. From now on, you don't have to worry about it. You don't ever have to close another drawer. I'm going to accept that as one of my jobs. Our drawer problem is over!"

From that day to this, open drawers have never bothered me. I feel no emotion, no hostility. I simply close them. That is my job. When I get home tonight, I can guarantee the open drawers will be waiting for me. I shall close them, and all will be well.

What am I suggesting by this illustration? That in marriage you will discover things that you do not like about your mate. It may be the way he hangs towels (or doesn't hang towels!). It may be the "classic rock" station he plays on the car radio . . . the way she tends to interrupt . . . the annoying way he has of forgetting people's names . . . the way she leaves her shoes all over for you to trip on.

The first course of action is to request change. (If you can change, why not? It is a small matter to make your partner happy.) However, I can assure you that there are some things that your mate either cannot or will not change. This is the point at which "love accepts many imperfections." You decide where the point of acceptance will come.

IN CLOSING

Some of you have had running battles for twenty years over things as simple as open drawers. Could this be the time to call a cease-fire and make a list of things that you will accept as imperfections? I do not want to discourage you, but your mate will never be perfect. He or she will never do everything that you desire.

Your best alternative is the acceptance of love!

Your Turn

1. *Having confessed your failures and accepted God's forgiveness and having asked your partner to forgive you, ask God to let you be His agent for loving your partner. Ask Him to fill you with His Spirit and His love. (God will answer this prayer because He has already told us that this is His will—see Ephesians 5:18, 25; Titus 2:3–4.)*

2. *Forget about your feelings. You do not have to feel anything to love your partner. Feelings may change because of your actions, but feelings should not dictate your actions. Choose to love your mate, no matter how you feel.*

3. *Express love to your mate by word or action once each day for the next month. Read again the sections "Loving with Words" and "Loving with Deeds." Perhaps you could begin with a compliment each day for the next week.*

4. *Do not allow your mate's reaction to stifle your love. Nothing your mate does can stop your love as long as you choose to love. Why stop when love is your greatest weapon for good and growth?*

5. *Consider the possibility of accepting in your mate some imperfection that has irritated you for years. If you decide to accept it, be sure to tell your mate. Such acceptance can be a positive step in your own emotional growth.*

6. *Few individuals can resist genuine, unconditional love for more than a year. Why not start today? Make this the greatest year of your marriage. Many have found that in less than a month, love has begotten love, and their whole marriage has been turned around.*

CHAPTER FOUR

"Listen to Me!"

WE LIVE IN AN AGE of noise and babble, both seen and heard. Talking heads on cable TV. The endless stream of email and text messages most of us get. The guy walking through the mall chattering on his cellphone. Bad piped-in music wherever we go. Noisy open offices. Kids at home! And the list goes on and on.

To be sure, we as a culture love to "communicate." Rare is the place where we can find silence and peace.

But what *kind* of communication? That is the question.

When we fail to communicate openly and meaningfully—indeed, when we fail to share our lives with our mates—we dam up the stream of life and tend to create a stagnant pool of self-pity. We feel alone because we are alone. We may still live in the same house, but we live as two lonely people rather than as a unit. This is precisely the opposite of what God intended. In the beginning He said, "It is not good for the man to be alone [cut off]" (Genesis 2:18). Many individuals have found themselves "cut off" in the midst of marriage. It is never good to be alone.

AN ACT OF THE WILL

Contrary to those lofty ideals that we had before marriage, free-flowing communication does not come naturally. On the other hand, neither is it, as some couples have concluded, impossible to attain. If we are to become one and enjoy that warm flow of life that is the deepest of all human satisfactions, we must communicate. We cannot know each other unless we confide in each other. The apostle Paul put his finger on this truth when he addressed the church at Corinth: "No one can know a person's thoughts except that person's own spirit, and no one can know God's thoughts except God's own Spirit" (1 Corinthians 2:11).

Just as we would never know what God is like if He had not chosen to communicate Himself through His Spirit, so we cannot know each other unless we choose to communicate. "I can read him like a book" may be true after fifty years of free communication, but it is not true in the early years of marriage.

No, your husband cannot read your mind, as you very well know. If you want him to be sensitive to your feelings, you must tell him how you are feeling! If you want your wife to be interested in what is going on in your world, you must let her in.

Communication is an act of the will. This is illustrated in 2 Corinthians 6:11, 13, where Paul says to the Corinthians, "Our hearts are open to you. . . . Open your hearts to us!"

We communicate or do not communicate by a deliberate act. We cannot truthfully say, "It's just my personality. I'm just not a 'great communicator'!"

Communication is basically an act of the will, not a matter of the personality.

Now, it is true that some of us have what might be called a "Dead Sea personality." We can have many thoughts, feelings, and experiences and be perfectly content not to express them to anyone. We feel no compulsion to talk. Others have the "babbling brook personality": everything that enters the mind comes out the mouth, and usually there is not a sixty-second lapse between the two. The "Dead Sea personality" will have greater difficulty expressing himself than will the "babbling brook." On the other hand, the "babbling brook" has the equally difficult problem of learning to listen.

Both talking and listening are required for effective communication. Each of us tends to lean toward one of these two extremes in basic personality orientation. Therefore, we each have our own difficulty in communication, but we can communicate. Communication is basically an act of the will, not a matter of the personality.

Our personalities may be an asset or a liability to communication, but they never render us bankrupt. Either I choose to share my heart, or I choose to keep the door closed. I cannot blame my personality, my mate's response, or anything else. If I live unto myself, I do so by choice and in deliberate disobedience to the command of God for oneness between marriage partners. Marriage cannot reach its ideal unless both partners choose to communicate.

BEYOND "FINE"

If we are having trouble communicating deeply with our spouses, it is easiest to begin with sharing the day-to-day events of our lives, then to move on to the deeper levels of communication. Those of us who are parents have all had the experience of our children coming home from some event—a field trip, say, or a church retreat—and responding with "Fine" to our question, "How did it go?" (Or sometimes their answer is, "I don't know"!)

Often we wait, and in time they choose to tell us "how it went." Or we ask gentle questions designed to elicit more than monosyllables.

How can we do this in marriage if we're not good at it? My suggestion to young marrieds and to others who have problems with this level of communication is to bend over backward for a few weeks to communicate the details: "Well, dear, I got on the train and found my usual seat . . . then I took out my phone and went on Instagram and saw pictures of my brother's vacation . . . When I got to work I pressed the elevator button and . . ."

Of course, I am speaking in hyperbole, but you get the point. Relate in great detail what is going on in your life. After a couple of days of this, you will be able to mention only the more important events of the day. More important, you can begin to express your *feelings* as well as simply talking about "what happened." The process of such sharing will bring a fresh sense of oneness to your mate. He/she will begin to feel a part of what you are doing.

It is also helpful for each partner to visit the location of the other's employment, if both are working. With a visual image of your work setting, your mate will be better able to identify with your world. Introduce each other to your close associates at work so that, when you come home and say, "Kevin was really in a bad mood today," your mate has a mental image of Kevin and what he must look like on a bad day.

A second level of communication is that of problem solving or decision making. Since an entire chapter is devoted to the decision-making process, I will not discuss this level of communication except to say that this is often the first point of conflict in marriage.

WHEN THE HEAT'S ON

The third level of communication is communicating when "the pressure's on." When the emotional temperature rises, reason fades, emotion ascends the throne, and chaos results. How do we prevent chaos and bring unity out of those pressure moments?

One warm August day many years ago, my wife-to-be and I made a visit to the minister who was to perform our wedding ceremony. We ate dinner under an aged oak tree, and he presented this bit of advice, which I have never forgotten: "When you are angry, take turns talking." He went on to explain that I should take three to five minutes to state my ideas on the issue while my wife remained silent (no butting in allowed). Then she should be given three to five minutes to state her understanding of the issue. This process should continue as long as necessary.

On that warm August day, I could not imagine that I would ever need to use such a strategy with the perfect wife God had given me. Why should I ever get that angry at her? That question was soon to be answered, and I was to become proficient at "taking turns." I have suggested the same to hundreds of couples since. Taking turns does not solve the problem, but it does cool down the heat so that you can get at the problem.

HOW TO TAKE TURNS

Let me suggest other guidelines for taking turns. When your partner is talking, you should be listening. One of the great discoveries of communication is the awesome power of the listening ear. Most of us have never reached our potential as listeners. James said, "You must all be quick to listen" (James 1:19). Talking is of little value unless someone is listening. When your spouse is talking, it is your turn to listen. Do not sit there and reload your guns. You cannot concentrate on what she is saying if you are marshaling your own forces. Your ideas will come back to you when it is your turn. Do not worry about your ideas. Concentrate on those of your mate.

Listen to the facts and the feelings being expressed. In light of what she is saying, try to understand how she came to feel that way. If you can understand, then a statement to that effect could be a powerful medication. "I can understand how you would feel that way; I really can. Let me explain my action as I saw it." Then take your turn at presenting the way things looked from your vantage point. When you are truly wrong, be ready to admit your wrongness, as we've already discussed. There is no value in rationalization.

Ask yourself, "What needs does my spouse have that I am not meeting?" Her feeling may be that you haven't done certain chores she's been asking you about for days—chores that may not be important to you but are important to her.

"It took a long time for my husband and me to come to terms on this one," said one wife recently. "Little things like getting the old newspapers out to the garage for recycling so they don't pile up around the house aren't a big deal to him, but they are to me because I hate clutter. It's kind of a visual thing. I finally said, 'Look, sweetie. It's important to me, and because you love me, you'll do it. It isn't hard to do, time-consuming, or expensive. So . . .' I don't think he'd ever thought of it quite that way before.

"Or he needs not to be interrupted, and I tend to interrupt because he takes time to pull his thoughts together—like a lot of guys, really. Again, I don't mind being interrupted. To me it's no big deal; I can pick up where I left off. I like lively give-and-take. To him it's disrespecting him. I'm trying to work at this, because it matters to him."

Love is considerate. What can you do about it? You have the potential for meeting the needs of your mate. If you accept this as your goal, you will be following the biblical admonition of Philippians 2:3–4: "Don't be selfish; don't try to impress others. Be humble, thinking of others as better than yourselves. Don't look out only for your own interests, but take an interest in others, too."

BREAKING DOWN THE BARRIERS

The picture of marital oneness is beautiful, but the creation of such a portrait is another matter. It requires your greatest creativity and energies, but few things in life are more rewarding. Because there are common barriers to communication, I want to give practical suggestions that may speak to your own problem.

"They Won't Open Up" — Without doubt, the most common complaint I hear from troubled couples is that one partner refuses to talk meaningfully. More often than not it is the husband who is the silent one. It would be unfair, however, to convey the idea that this is characteristic only of males. Many women also find it more comfortable to draw the curtains of the soul. Let me say first of all that this tendency to keep things inside should not be viewed as a mental disorder. I have known husbands who have recognized their own reticence to open their hearts to anyone, their wives included, and who have allowed the problem to lead to depression and self-deprivation. Their conclusion has been that they are hopelessly mentally ill. Such is not the case.

We all have strengths and weaknesses in our personalities. Though we cannot correct the past, we are masters of the future. Throughout childhood, for whatever reason, we may have developed a withdrawn, inwardly directed personality, but that does not mean that we cannot learn to open our lives and experience the joy of unity with our mates. Any pattern that has developed can also be altered. We must decide that marital oneness is worth the pain of alteration. (And I assure you that it is.)

As one husband said, "Please don't stop asking questions just because I give a short answer."

A beginning step to communication is to discuss the problem with your spouse. Sit down with her in a comfortable setting, and in your own words say, "Darling, I know that the unity of our marriage is not what it could be. I know also that one of our big problems is my reluctance to talk with you. I keep things inside; I have difficulty saying what I really think or feel. I know that this makes it hard on you because you cannot read my mind. I really want to grow in this area, and I am asking for your help. I am not sure what you can do to help, but maybe you have some ideas." Give your mate a chance to respond. Perhaps she does have some ideas.

Continue by telling her some of the things that you believe make it difficult for you to be open. Tell her that when she keeps asking you to "talk more," she simply makes it harder for you to get started. Perhaps she could ask questions about specific matters. As one husband said, "Please don't stop asking questions just because I give a short answer. I really want to say more, but I just can't get it all out with the first question. Keep the questions coming and, it is hoped, I'll keep talking."

Perhaps your spouse could help by asking your advice from time to time. Most of us talk more readily if someone asks for specific advice, especially if we believe that the person really wants it. Perhaps, also, if she or he would develop some interest in your vocation or your hobbies, you would have something else in common about which you could talk. Read a news magazine, watch a home-improvement channel together, take an evening school course. If it enhances oneness, it is time and money well invested.

The issues may go deeper than this, though. Maybe there's a wound from the past that needs healing. If it is still on your mind, you need to be open so that your partner can have a chance to correct it. No failure is worth a lifetime of misery. You must be willing to confess and forgive. If you have difficulty verbalizing the problem, then write it in a letter and ask him to read it in your presence. Then discuss the matter. Sometimes you can say in writing what you have difficulty expressing aloud.

Perhaps, also, your mate could help by examining his or her own flow of conversation. Maybe he is talking so much that you have no opportunity. Many wives and husbands ask a question and then proceed to answer it. The other partner feels unneeded. Some could profit greatly by applying the advice of James: "You must all be quick to listen, slow to speak" (James 1:19). You have heard the story of the little girl who was writing a paper on Abraham Lincoln. She asked her mother for help, and her mother, knowing her husband was a Civil War buff, said, "Ask your dad." The girl said, "I didn't want to know *that* much."

If you believe discussion of other areas would help communication, confide in each other. After all, your discussion is on communication. You are admitting your difficulty and looking for help, so any suggestion should be considered. Perhaps your sexual needs are not being met, and you have developed a very negative attitude toward your mate. You have never discussed it, but this may be a real barrier to your communication in other areas. This is the time to speak of it. It cannot hurt. It may help.

May I suggest, as a conclusion to this conversation about your problems in communication, that you join in prayer. You may or may not be able to pray aloud, but certainly you can pray silently. If it is to be silent prayer, then agree to hold hands while praying and say "Amen" when you have finished.

"I Have Such a Temper"— Uncontrolled anger is certainly a barrier to communication. It is difficult if not impossible to communicate when one is angry. The capacity for anger, however, must not be seen as an evil. It is the emotion of anger against injustice and inequity that gives rise to social reform. Jesus Himself was angry upon occasion (Mark 3:5).

Most of our anger, however, does not arise from a concern for righteousness but from a self-centered heart. Someone has rubbed us the wrong way, or we did not get our way. Such anger is condemned in Scripture (Ephesians 4:31). Even a righteous anger can very easily lead to wrong actions. Therefore, Paul warns us in Ephesians 4:26, "Don't sin by letting anger control you." We must not allow anger to control us and lead us to wrong actions.

The emotion of anger may be beyond our control, but our actions in response to anger are not. We have the ability to control anger instead of being controlled by it. We cannot rightfully excuse rash behavior by simply saying, "I have a temper." We all have tempers, and we all have the responsibility to deal with our tempers.

In marital conflict, how then am I to control my anger? I suggest the simple technique of withdrawing for evaluation. When you feel anger rising (all of us are aware of when that is happening to us), at that moment move to control it. A simple statement such as "I can feel myself getting angry. I don't want to get angry, and I know you do not want me to get angry. So, let's agree to stop discussing this until I can get my feelings under control." (I am not talking about days, but perhaps minutes or at most a few hours.) The biblical admonition is "Don't let the sun go down while you are still angry" (Ephesians 4:26). This is not an avoidance of the conflict but a temporary withdrawal for the purpose of controlling emotions.

Having withdrawn from the source of heat, evaluate your thoughts, actions, and feelings with God. Never try to do this alone, or you will come to the wrong conclusions. "Lord, why would I get so upset over this matter?" might be an appropriate prayer. Admit and confess selfish motives, wrong attitudes, or any other failure—first to God, then to your mate.

With the emotion calmed, come back to discussing the problem, perhaps using the each-take-a-turn approach mentioned earlier. There are answers to all problems. Following your anger with harsh, cutting words or physical abuse only compounds the problem. It never solves it.

Anger may well reveal an area of your relationship that needs attention. If you respond constructively, it can stimulate growth in oneness. If, however, you allow anger to control you, it will lead to separation, not oneness. Anger always drives apart. Control of anger may well bring you closer together.

> *Selfishness is the greatest barrier to oneness, and we are all afflicted with the disease.*

"He's So Selfish"— "But my husband is so selfish," someone says. "Even when he does communicate, it is to demand his own way. I am always wrong. 'Sit down and let me tell you how things are going to be' is his idea of communication."

Selfishness is the greatest barrier to oneness, and we are all afflicted with the disease. We are our own greatest enemy in attaining marital unity. By nature we lean in the opposite direction: "My side always appears right to me. Otherwise, it would not be my side. You don't think I would choose the wrong side, do you?"

It is an awareness of human nature that will help us at this point. Recognizing this chink in our armor will help us evaluate every situation in a more realistic manner. I can expect myself to be selfish because this is my nature. But as a Christian, I have a new nature—the very real presence of the Holy Spirit in my life. Therefore, I have a choice. I do not have to bow to my old selfish nature. I have the option of choosing to cooperate with the Holy Spirit in doing the unselfish thing.

The opposite of selfishness is love, biblical love, which is self-giving and unconditional. This is the greatest gift I have to offer my mate. But I am not free to offer such love until I have *decided against selfishness*. The choice is mine.

It is true that you cannot deal with the selfishness of your mate. You can deal only with your own. If you deal with your own, however, you are giving your mate a model to emulate. (Most of us would respond positively to a loving model.) When you no longer fight the selfishness of your mate, you are free to concentrate upon the defeat of your own selfishness.

"I Don't Want to Hurt Her" — Many husbands and wives have refrained from expressing themselves because they did not want to hurt their mates. They have believed that if they were honest, it would be more than the partners could stand. Thus, they are content to live with limited unity rather than splinter the relationship. The intent is worthy, and most of us have felt this tension at one time or another. Yet we cannot grow and mature in our relationship without taking on adult responsibilities—which are sometimes challenging.

I do not mean that you should hit your mate with your whole tale of woe thirty minutes before dinner on Friday evening. A time and place should be selected carefully. There is also the principle of constructive communication as opposed to destructive explosion. Romans 14:19 (NIV) suggests, "Let us therefore make every effort to do what leads to peace and to mutual edification." The word *edify*, as we've seen, means to "build up." Your objective must be clearly in mind—to build up your mate. "Love edifies" (1 Corinthians 8:1 NASB).

I am not encouraging the emptying of your negative garbage upon your mate's head in the name of honesty. The Christian plan is to speak the truth in love (Ephesians 4:15), and love edifies. We speak the truth, but we seek to say it in such a way as to build up, rather than to destroy.

A good question to ask is "What is my motive in saying this?" Are you doing it out of a bitter heart that wants to be vindictive? Then it is wrong and will drive you apart rather than draw you together. All of us have negative thoughts and feelings toward our mates at certain times. Honesty does not compel us to express all these feelings. We must allow these feelings to go through the sieve of "edification." If they come out as building blocks—great! Express them! If they come out as bombs, then defuse them before you have destroyed the very thing that you most desire.

Having said this, I want to remind you that certain aspects of building up another are painful. Personal growth does not come without pain. And genuine love moves out to stimulate growth even if it must be accompanied with pain. No one enjoys pain, and your mate will not likely be joyful over your expression of truth, but if such pain can bring growth, it is worthwhile. Surgery is never a pleasing thought, but the result may be life itself. All of us need emotional, social, and spiritual surgery along the way, and our mates may well be the chosen surgeons.

Certainly you will want to express your own disappointments and frustrations. One is not always happy or satisfied. A mature marriage will provide acceptance even when the mate is "out of sorts." That is never the time for criticism but rather for acceptance and understanding.

Never use "honesty" as a license to pour out all your unhappiness and blame it on your mate. Remember, happiness or unhappiness is a state of mind that you choose for yourself. It may be helped or hindered by your mate's attitudes and actions, but the choice is yours.

At the same time, you must not be overprotective of your mate. What your mate needs is not another mother or father but a full partner who loves him enough to speak the truth in love.

Weigh your medication carefully. Do not give an overdose. None of us can face all our weaknesses on the same day. Medicine must be taken at regular intervals, not all at once. Find the best time—never when one is hungry, or late at night. Ask your mate if he thinks he could take a little constructive criticism. Do not give it unless he is ready. Make sure that your criticism is something to which your mate can respond positively.

Couple your criticism with compliments. The biblical pattern for criticism is found in Revelation 2:2, 4. Christ said to the church at Ephesus, "I know all the things you do. I have seen your hard work and your patient endurance. . . . But I have this complaint against you." He then proceeded to give them one criticism.

Three compliments, one complaint is the pattern. It helps if the compliments are given in the same area as the criticism. Even before you give the compliments, however, wait to be invited to confront an issue. For example, let's say that my wife wants to criticize me about leaving hairs in the sink. She might begin by saying, "Honey, do you feel like you could take a constructive criticism tonight?" Now she has given me the option of saying "Yes" or "No." If I say "No," I can almost guarantee you I will come back in less than an hour and say, "About that criticism, what did you have in mind? I'm dying to know." And she says, "No, it can wait until tomorrow or even next week. You let me know when you're feeling like it." I will probably respond, "I'm feeling better now."

Now she begins—with compliments, "Before I make my request, let me tell you some things I like about you. First of all, I appreciate the fact that you always throw your dirty clothes in the hamper. I've talked to other women who say their husbands leave clothes lying all over the house. You've never done that. Secondly, I appreciate the fact that you got the bugs off my windshield last night. I love it when you get the bugs off my windshield. And thirdly, I want you to know how much I appreciate the fact that you quietly take care of the online bill paying so we're never behind.

"What I'm saying is 'I really like you' and there's one thing, if you would change it, that would make me even happier."

By now, she has my full attention and because I feel appreciated by her, I am ready to respond to her suggestion. So she says, "When I go into the bathroom and find hairs all over the sink, it irritates me greatly. So, if possible, I'd like to request that before you leave the bathroom, you get the hairs out of the sink."

I will confess this conversation is not fiction, and I am the best sink cleaner you'll ever find.

The compliments give me the assurance that I am not a failure. Basically, I am doing a pretty good job, so I am motivated to continue growth. If, however, you give me the criticism without the compliments, I am likely to give up. "I do everything I can to please him/her, and what do I get! Another criticism! I give up!" These are likely to be my thoughts.

"I Know That I Lack Self-Confidence" — Many of us struggle with long-term, deep-seated feelings of inadequacy—even though on the surface we may look confident and competent. We look back at a string of failures and find our successes hard to remember. We view ourselves as threatened by every social encounter. Thus, when we come to marriage, we find it difficult to express our ideas for fear of further rejection and failure. James Dobson observes that "Lack of self-esteem produces more symptoms of psychiatric disorders than any other factor yet identified."[1] He notes that our culture's value system exalts beauty, brains, and athletic ability.[2] If we have failed in these three areas (most of which are beyond our control), then we see ourselves as failures.

But your self-concept could be wrong. So you may not be a supermodel or a Stanford graduate or be able to sink a putt like Tiger Woods—where does that leave you? It leaves you with the rest of us normal mortals made in the image of God. Hundreds around you have fought those same feelings of inadequacy and have won. So can you.

Surely, you have weaknesses. Surely, you have failed. But you also have strengths, and you can succeed in many things. You may not be able to pass the MCAT entrance exam to medical school, but you know how to get a website up and running. You may not look like a size 0, but you're outgoing and likable and have great artistic flair. Your skills are not the same as others, nor should they be. God does not run a cookie factory where we all come out looking alike. His is a snowflake factory, noted for variety.

Be your best self under God's direction. Utilize your abilities; do not worry about those things that are beyond your control. You are a worthy person because you are made in the image of God. Your worth is not determined by what you have done or have not done. You can accomplish worthy goals. Do not let your emotions push you around. Admit your feelings of inadequacy to

God, but thank Him that you "can do everything through Christ, who gives [you] strength" (Philippians 4:13).

How can a marriage partner help a mate with low self-esteem? By encouraging him or her to accept the past and to concentrate on the future—and by the assurance of love and concern. That is what marriage is all about. One does not have to bear his burden alone (Galatians 6:2). James Dobson offers a touching picture of such spousal encouragement:

Life has been tough and you've had your share of suffering. To this point, you've faced your problems without much human support and there have been times when your despair has been overwhelming. Let me, now, share that burden. From this moment forward, I am interested in you as a person: you deserve and shall have my respect. As best as possible, I want you to quit worrying about your troubles. Instead, confide them to me. Our concentration will be on the present and the future, and together we will seek appropriate solutions.[3]

When a mate makes such a statement to a partner, he/she is conveying acceptance, love, understanding, encouragement, and direction. It calls for a positive attitude rather than despair. This is always the attitude for growth.

IN CLOSING

Healthy, meaningful communication is not a luxury; it is a necessity. There can be no unity without such communication. The barriers to communication are formidable but not unconquerable. The key is your own will to communicate. Motivated with the vision of oneness in marriage, you must choose to communicate regardless of your emotions and past failures. The process will not be without pain, but then pain is the handmaiden of growth. The following suggestions are designed to help you, if you will!

Your Turn

Look at your own marriage and ask honestly: "Am I happy with the degree of communication that we have attained?" (If you are not, keep reading.)

1. *Write down the areas where you feel communication is most needed in your marriage.*

2. *Who is the most talkative in your marriage?*

3. *If you find it very difficult to communicate your thoughts and feelings to your mate, consider an open discussion as suggested in the section entitled "My Mate Won't Talk." (Certainly it will be hard to get started, but, as an ancient Chinese sage said, "The journey of a thousand miles begins with a first step.")*

4. *Reread each section of this chapter, and write down after each section ways in which you believe you could make a contribution toward growing communication with your mate. Seek to implement these on a regular basis.*

5. *Read each section aloud with your mate and discuss what you see about yourself in that particular section. (Do not mention what you see about your mate unless he/she asks you to do so.)*

6. *Ask your mate if he/she would like you to help in any area of communication. (Do not press the issue.)*

CHAPTER FIVE

Who Takes Care of What?

AMY AND DAN are just back from a honeymoon in Maui. They've both gone back to work and are excited about their first evening together in their new condo. Amy arrives home thirty minutes before Dan and, after greeting their cat, decides to begin dinner—her first as a married person! Before she has the water boiling, Dan walks in the door, goes straight to the kitchen, and sweeps her off her feet with a warm embrace and a passionate kiss. Before she has recovered, he is on his phone, playing a game.

When dinner is ready, Amy calls him, and he bounces in with a big smile and says, "Boy, does this smell good!" A normal amount of chatter follows, mostly the relating of various comments of friends at the office, and dinner is ended. Dan excuses himself and rushes off to watch NCAA basketball, while Amy proceeds to clear the table and wash dishes. By and by they get together and have a tender evening.

The next evening the procedure is much the same as that described above. The third evening brings Act III (the same as Acts I and II). By now Amy is glaring at Dan, who is obliviously talking on the phone to his brother about North Carolina's chances this year. When he hangs up, she's ready—and unloads.

Dan is dumbfounded. What's he done wrong? "But you like to cook," he protests. "You've always said so. You cooked for me when we were dating."

What Dan doesn't add is that his mother, a full-time homemaker, always assumed kitchen duty (and everything else inside the home), while his dad retreated to his den.

And what Amy doesn't add is that when she was growing up, her dad, an illustrator who worked at home, shared many household tasks with her mom, a retail manager. Neither she nor Dan could articulate these expectations completely. It's simply what they observed growing up—therefore, each of them carried the unspoken assumption that this was the "right" way to do things.

Amy and Dan are demonstrating what happens in most homes sometime during the first three months of marriage, as the couple realizes that they have never agreed upon the answer to that all-important question: "How do you divide up chores?" Even in today's world, at some point somebody has to clean up after somebody else. Somebody has to make sure the rent is paid. In the interest of orderly living, life runs more smoothly if each spouse takes on certain agreed-upon tasks, rather than endlessly having to renegotiate: This week I'll make a Target run if you'll clean out the cat's box. Past generations tended to divide responsibilities very traditionally, but as women moved into the workforce in increasing numbers and societal views changed, the image of Dad reading his paper while Mom vacuumed under his feet went out with black-and-white TV.

SORTING THROUGH SOME ASSUMPTIONS

But even today, most of us bring certain assumptions to the "table" of marriage: Men (so we assume) fix things, kill bugs, grill, and deal with anything having to do with cars or garbage. Women (regardless of whether they work or not) keep the home attractive, doing the little things like wiping the stove, and making sure there is soap in the shower, and doing the big things like making the final decisions about decorating. Women also keep the family schedule, handle social arrangements, and know where the kids are supposed to be when.

How, then, do we sort through these assumptions? Many conflicts could be eliminated if the couple would take time before marriage to discuss and agree upon responsibilities. Normally the problem is not the inability to agree upon responsibilities but rather the failure to even discuss the matter. But even marital veterans can benefit from a periodic check, evaluating whether their way of divvying up chores is working (or whether a given task has to be done at all!).

First, though, we need to return to our idea of oneness in marriage—and God's intention.

TEAM ADAM AND EVE

In the very beginning, God assigned to Adam and Eve an objective: "God blessed them and said, 'Be fruitful and multiply. Fill the earth and govern it. Reign over the fish in the sea, the birds in the sky, and all the animals that scurry along the ground'" (Genesis 1:28).

Both husband and wife had work to do. They were called by God to reproduce themselves physically and to govern, or have dominion over, the earth with all its creatures. Both were to be a part of accomplishing the goal, but obviously they could not both play the same role. Physically, the woman was to be the childbearer, but in this process man was to play a vital role. God's pattern is unity. It is always God's plan that husband and wife work as a team. Physical birth demands such teamwork and is a model for all of life.

Just as physical reproduction requires the cooperative work of husband and wife, each playing a different role but each necessary and both working together as a unit, so in all other areas the pattern is to have varying responsibilities but unity of purpose. The players on an athletic team do not all do the same tasks, but they do have the same objective. Thus, the husband and wife do not perform identical roles, but they work toward a common objective as a team commissioned by God.

An allusion to the diversity of roles for Adam and Eve is seen in Genesis 3, where God pronounces judgment upon them for their sin:

Then he said to the woman, "I will sharpen the pain of your pregnancy, and in pain you will give birth. And you will desire to control your husband, but he will rule over you." And to the man he said, "Since you listened to your wife and ate from the tree whose fruit I commanded you not to eat, the ground is cursed because of you. All your life you will struggle to scratch a living from it. It will grow thorns and thistles for you, though you will eat of its grains. By the sweat of your brow will you have food to eat until you return to the ground from which you were made. For you were made from dust, and to dust you will return. (Genesis 3:16–19)

God's judgment upon Eve was related to pain in childbirth. Childbirth was certainly a role unique to Eve. This judgment did not affect man's role in the reproductive process. When God placed a specific judgment upon Adam, He chose the earth, for Adam was a farmer. Thorns and thistles were to make the process of cultivation more difficult.

Both of these judgments would stand as a constant reminder of the results of sin, and each judgment was tailored to fit. That is, Eve's judgment met her in a role that was uniquely hers, and Adam's judgment faced him every day in the fields as he performed his major responsibility of providing food for his family.

The biblical emphasis in child rearing is always on "parents," not "mothers."

If Eve was to accomplish her role in reaching God's objective ("Be fruitful and multiply"), then obviously she would not be able to till the fields. Since Adam's role in reproduction was different, he was free to focus his energies on the second aspect of God's objective, that of governing the earth and having dominion over other living creatures. The emphasis, then, was upon the wife as the childbearer and the husband as the provider.

These roles are not to be thought of as airtight compartments. Anyone who knows anything about an agrarian economy knows that the farmer's wife plays a vital role in the success of the farm. Also, Adam certainly had responsibilities related to child rearing. The biblical emphasis in child rearing is always on "parents," not "mothers." What we do have in this chapter is an introduction to the idea of varying responsibilities within marriage, with an emphasis on teamwork in reaching God's objectives.

WORK, FAMILY, AND MAKING CHOICES

Then there is the famous Proverbs 31 woman we are all familiar with:

Who can find a virtuous and capable wife? She is more precious than rubies. Her husband can trust her, and she will greatly enrich his life. She brings him good, not harm, all the days of her life. She finds wool and flax and busily spins it. She is like a merchant's ship, bringing her food from afar. She gets up before dawn to prepare breakfast for her household and plan the day's work for her servant girls. She goes to inspect a field and buys it; with her earnings she plants a vineyard. She is energetic and strong, a hard worker. She makes sure her dealings are profitable; her lamp burns late into the night. Her hands are busy spinning thread, her fingers twisting fiber. She extends a helping hand to the poor and opens her arms to the needy. She has no fear of winter for her household, for everyone has warm clothes. She makes her own bedspreads. She dresses in fine linen and purple gowns. Her husband is well known at the city gates, where he sits with the other civic leaders. She makes belted linen garments and sashes to sell to the merchants. She is clothed with strength and dignity, and she laughs without fear of the future. When she speaks, her words are wise, and she gives instructions with kindness. She carefully watches everything in her household and suffers nothing from laziness. Her children stand and bless her. Her husband praises her. (vv. 10–28)

No one could read this chapter and conclude that the wife's role is to be limited to childbearing. Yet one profound impression is made—for this wife, the "center of gravity" was her home. She engaged in numerous and diverse activities: sewing, cooking, buying fields, planting vineyards, making and selling fine linen and garments, caring for the poor and needy, and speaking with wisdom and kindness. This wife certainly contributed economically to the home. Yet all of these were directed toward the well-being of her family: her husband (vv. 11–12), her children (vv. 15, 21, 27), and herself (v. 22).

The results of such a life? "Her children stand and bless her. Her husband praises her" (v. 28).

I believe it is this picture Paul had in mind when he wrote that the older women were to instruct the younger women to "work in their homes" (Titus 2:5). This does not mean that the Christian wife must confine herself to any particular set of household duties, but it does mean that her family must be central in all her activities. When faced with a decision regarding a new responsibility, the questions ought always to be, how will it affect my family? My husband? My children? Myself? Our relationship with each other?

It is important to note, however, that how these convictions are lived out will vary from family to family. Many working women make extraordinary sacrifices in this regard, from the professional who opts for at-home freelance work (at considerable cost to the family income) to the mother who comes home at night after a long day and spends hours helping her kids with their homework, putting her own rest and refreshment on hold. Sometimes it means returning to the workforce so that the family may afford Christian college for their children. (Note, too, that the New Testament also has many references to "working" women—tentmaking Priscilla, whom we meet in Acts and again in Romans, 1 Corinthians, and 2 Timothy; Lydia, "a merchant of expensive purple cloth" (Acts 16:14); and do not forget the women who, Luke 8 tells us, traveled with and contributed financially to the ministry of Jesus and the Twelve.

What of the husband's responsibility? First Timothy 5:8 says, "But those who won't care for their relatives, especially those in their own household, have denied the true faith. Such people are worse than unbelievers." In the context, this passage is dealing with a man's responsibility to care for widows in his family, but certainly, if he is to care for widows, he has the same responsibility for his more immediate family.

GOD THE PROVIDER

Jesus, of course, consistently refers to God as His Father. Here is His picture of God as Provider:

> You parents—if your children ask for a loaf of bread, do you give them a stone instead? Or if they ask for a fish, do you give them a snake? Of course not! So if you sinful people know how to give good gifts to your children, how much more will your heavenly Father give good gifts to those who ask him. (Matthew 7:9–11)

If you wanted to describe God's role as Father in one word, which word would you choose? I would choose the word *Provider.* He has provided everything necessary for life and godliness (2 Peter 1:3). Not only has He given life, but He sustains life and meets all our needs.

That does not mean that the wife does not take initiative and responsibility in making provision for the family. Proverbs 31 dispels that idea. Husband and wife are a team, and they work together, but the scriptural pattern is for the husband to take the basic responsibility for meeting the physical needs of his family.

WORKING WIVES, INVOLVED DADS

Certainly there are many families in which, for various reasons, the wife must assume the role of principal earner. And, increasingly in recent years, with shifts in the economy and disappearance of job security, women have picked up the earning slack from husbands struggling with unemployment or underemployment. God will give strength and grace to these wives. Such a wife should, however, help her husband to see his role in the relationship and continue to respect and encourage him. Remember, husband and wife constitute a team, and everyone on a team must share responsibility.

In the same way, we have become much more aware in recent years of the importance of involved, committed fathers—and the cost to family and society when this does not happen. One boomer husband recently reflected, "When I was growing up, my dad was always traveling for his business. He didn't do anything around the house and wasn't very involved in my brother's and my lives, except for taking us places like the circus every now and then. I vowed that when I grew up I'd be different with my own family." Many men his age and younger share the same commitment.

The physical role of the mother in childbearing and nurturing is essential, but the child also needs the warm emotional involvement of the father. The child needs both parents; the father must be as concerned for the welfare of the child as is the mother. Fellowship and training of children cannot be delegated to the mother exclusively. Many Christian fathers have made this fatal mistake. Husband and wife are members of a team and must function as teammates.

Today, of course, the majority of wives work outside the home. Before the children come, it is relatively easy to negotiate what both husband and wife agree to be a fair distribution of responsibilities. Utilizing each of their interests and expertise, they agree on who will do what. Occasionally, they choose to "help" each other with their assigned tasks, and love flows freely between the two of them.

However, when the children arrive, there is a whole new dynamic. First of all, children require intensive care. Except for the hours when they are sleeping, they must have constant supervision. Each stage of childhood brings on additional areas of responsibility for parenting. How do we fit all of these responsibilities into the neat grid we had worked out before the children came? The reality is, we don't. Children call for a whole new responsibility contract. It's time to go back to the drawing table and renegotiate a fair and equitable arrangement that will allow the two of you to function as a team, utilizing your strengths to accomplish the tasks that both of you desire—being good parents as well as maintaining a healthy marriage.

FINDING A BALANCE

Recently, I spent some time with John and Ellen, who are in their late thirties and have three children. He is a medical doctor and she is a nurse, though she only works part-time since the first child arrived. I asked, "How do the two of you negotiate the responsibilities of parenting and household management?"

John smiled and said, "Sometimes, I'm afraid we don't do a very good job."

Ellen agreed, adding, "We're doing much better now than we did when we only had one child. Our first baby changed our lives so dramatically, I could not believe it. I had planned to go back to work full-time when the baby was three months old, but to be honest, I guess it was my maternal instincts, but I simply could not walk away and leave my baby every morning. That's when John and I agreed that I would go to a part-time schedule, but we still had a lot of details to work out. When the children were preschoolers, we had someone come in and care for the children when we were away. Now that they are all in school, I work my schedule so that I can be home when the children arrive in the afternoon.

"John has been great to help with all the things that have to be done around the house."

"I never dreamed that I would be doing laundry and cleaning the toilet," John added. "But I have to admit, it gives me a great sense of accomplishment, and I know that Ellen really appreciates what I do."

"He even cooks sometimes—only if it's basic stuff," Ellen said.

"I'm pretty good with hamburgers and hot dogs!" John said. "I did try macaroni the other night and it turned out pretty well."

"Our biggest challenge is finding time for each other," he continued. "We want to be involved in the lives of our children, and I think we are doing a pretty good job. But sometimes, we realize that we don't have enough time for just the two of us. We work at it, and sometimes we have to make hard decisions.

Last weekend, for example, I said no to a medical conference so that the two of us could have a weekend together. My folks came and kept the children. It was great to have three days with just the two of us."

WORKING AS A TEAM

It was obvious to me that John and Ellen had a vision for working as a team. And although it was a constant challenge, they were making every effort to be involved in the lives of their children and to maintain a growing marriage.

As a team, the husband and wife are to work together under God to determine the roles each will play so that together they may accomplish God's purposes for their union. The specific roles will vary from family to family and may change within the same family from time to time, but the roles should be agreeable to each partner. Accepting differing roles does not destroy identity but enhances it. As husband and wife, the couple is walking together toward the accepted goal.

In my opinion, the gifts and abilities of the partners should be considered when determining responsibilities. One may be more qualified than the other. Since you are on the same team, why not use the player best qualified in that area? In my own life, I would hate to imagine the chaos that would result if I bought the groceries. That is my wife's department, and she is highly qualified. For other couples, however, the husband may be particularly equipped for that task.

None of the above should be taken to mean that once a responsibility is accepted the other spouse should never help with that task. Let us say that the husband accepts the responsibility for vacuuming the floor every Thursday. This does not mean that the wife should never help him. Love wants to help and often will. What the acceptance of that responsibility does mean is that if the wife does not help her husband with the vacuuming, he will not be hurt. He is not expecting her to vacuum, because that is his duty. If she does help, he takes it as an act of love, and indeed it is.

IN CLOSING

The Scriptures do not tell us how to settle arguments about who does what—but they do encourage us to *agree* upon an answer. Amos once asked, "Do two walk together unless they have agreed to do so?" (3:3 NIV). The answer is, "No, not very far and not very well." Agreement upon responsibilities is a relatively simple matter, but if it is overlooked, problems may burst forth like lava from a volcano.

Your Turn

1. *In your marriage, who has the basic responsibility for providing financially?*

   _____ *Wife*   _____ *Husband*   _____ *Shared*

   Are you satisfied with the present arrangement? If no, write a brief description of the changes you would like to see.

2. *Without discussing it with your spouse, make a list of the items you consider to be your responsibility around the house. Make a separate list of those items you consider to be his/her responsibility. Include everything and be as specific as possible.*

3. *Have your spouse read this chapter and complete assignments 1 and 2 above.*

4. *At an agreed-upon time, show your lists to each other. You may find:*

   a. that you completely agree upon your roles.

   b. that you have specific items upon which you disagree (there is some area of confusion as to who has responsibility for what).

   c. that you agree on very little—thus, this is an area of real marital conflict.

5. *Whatever you find, use this time to discuss and evaluate your roles. What are you doing that you believe your mate is better qualified to do? Would he/she be willing to accept this responsibility? Let him/her try it for one month.*

6. *Do not ever believe that responsibilities cannot be changed. If conflict arises over roles, it is time for discussion and evaluation.*

CHAPTER SIX

Decisions, Decisions

SHOULD WE GO to grad school? Start a business? Have kids right away or get a dog? What color should we paint the living room? Where should we live when we retire? There is no end to the decisions we need to make in marriage. And it's important that the decisions be mutually agreed upon.

"The first real argument we ever had a few months after we were married was when my husband came home one day with a table he had spent fifty dollars on," one wife recalled. "I just lost it. It seemed like such a betrayal of trust. I mean, I actually liked the table. But I was working, and he was in school, and we had to watch our money. It was then that we agreed that we would consult on any purchase fifty dollars or up. And we've held to that."

As noted earlier, many couples who seem to have no difficulty communicating before marriage find communication coming to a standstill after marriage. The basic reason for this change is that, before marriage, no decision had to be made. They talked freely about any issue and then departed, each to do their own thing. After marriage, however, they are attempting to experience oneness, and decisions must be made that will affect both partners. Because they cannot agree on the decision, communication grinds to a halt, and a wall of separation begins to grow between them.

Sociologists and family counselors admit that one of the greatest problems in marriage is the decision-making process. Visions of democracy dance in the minds of many young couples, but when there are only two voting members, democracy often results in deadlock. Few still hold to the old autocratic system where the husband rules "with a rod of iron" and the wife is more of a child than a partner—or to a matriarchal system where the mother calls all the plays from the sideline, and the husband is at most the quarterback, running the plays.

What then are we to do? How shall we make decisions? Most newly married couples assume that decisions will take care of themselves. They anticipate no great problems in this area. Such illusions will soon be shattered. I remember the wife who said, "I never dreamed that we would argue with each other. Before marriage, we seemed so compatible."

Does the Bible offer any help? If we wanted to follow the best possible pattern of decision making, what would it be? I want to suggest that the best example we have for decision making among equals is God Himself.

WE THREE

As we've seen, God has revealed Himself as a Trinity. This Trinitarian God has made many decisions, some of which are recorded in the Bible. From the original "Let us make human beings in our image" (Genesis 1:26) to the final invitation of the Trinity in Revelation 22, God has made decisions. How were these decisions made?

Our information is limited, but in Matthew 26:36–46 we get to look in on a communication session between the Son and the Father. Jesus was facing the cross and, naturally, was feeling physical and emotional pressure. In these verses, we find Him expressing fully His feelings and thoughts to the Father. "My Father! If it is possible, let this cup of suffering be taken away from me" (v. 39). This is not meant to be a complete record of the prayer but rather its theme. There was no holding back, no facade, but utter openness with the Father. Three times the prayer was repeated, and each time Jesus concluded, "Yet

I want your will to be done, not mine" (v. 39; cf. vv. 42, 44).

Was this fatalism? Not at all. Jesus simply recognized the Father as the leader. Granted, the decision of the cross had been made in eternity past, for Jesus is "the Lamb that was slain from the creation of the world" (Revelation 13:8 NIV). But now, as He faced the cross in time and space, He voiced His human feelings to the Father.

Another verse explains this relationship even more clearly. In 1 Corinthians 11:3, Paul says, "But there is one thing I want you to know: The head of every man is Christ, the head of woman is man, and the head of Christ is God." That last phrase—"the head of Christ is God"—is overlooked by many. Paul is obviously referring to God the Father.

You might say, "I thought the Father and the Son were equal." They are! Yet within the perfect unity of the Godhead, there is order, and the Father is revealed as the leader. If we can understand something of the nature of this divine model, that is, how the Father relates to the Son and how the Son relates to the Father, then we will have a better understanding of what it means for the man to be the "head" of the woman.

EQUAL IN VALUE

Is the Father more valuable than the Son? Is a man more valuable than a woman? Is the Father more intelligent than the Son? Are men more intelligent than women? The obvious answer to these questions is no. The Father and the Son are equal in every respect. But equality does not mean that there are no distinctions. It was the Son who died on the cross, not the Father. Are men and women equal in value? Yes! Say it loudly and clearly. Let no one question where the Bible stands on this issue. Both males and females were made in the image of God and are of equal value.

Does equality mean they are identical? No. There are differences, but differences do not mean deficiencies. When God indicates that the man is to be the head of the woman, He is simply establishing order for a relationship among equals, a relationship that is pictured by God Himself.

Is it conceivable that the Father would ever force the Son to do anything against His will? Is it conceivable that a husband who followed this pattern would ever force his wife to do anything against her will? Headship does not mean dictatorship. Would the Son ever walk off to "do His own thing" without consulting the Father? "Unthinkable," you say. Would a wife ever walk off to "do her own thing" without consulting her husband? I know that God is perfect, and that we are imperfect; therefore, we do not always do what we know to be right. We must, however, understand the pattern to which we are called.

The biblical concept of man as the "head of the house" has perhaps been the most exploited concept of the Bible. Christian husbands, full of self-will, have made all kinds of foolish demands of their wives under the authority of "The Bible says . . ." Headship does not mean that the husband has the right to make all the decisions and inform the wife of what is going to be done. That is unthinkable if one looks seriously at the model of God the Father and God the Son.

IN SEARCH OF ONENESS

What, then, is the biblical pattern for decision making? Let us allow the conversation between Jesus and the Father that occurred in Gethsemane just prior to the crucifixion to be our example. "My Father! If it is possible, let this cup of suffering be taken away from me. Yet I want your will to be done, not mine" (Matthew 26:39).

The pattern seems to be a discussion of ideas and feelings—expressed in honesty and love—with the husband as the recognized leader. The objective is always oneness in our decisions. The Trinity knows perfect unity in every decision. As imperfect beings, we may not always be able to attain the ideal but that must always be our goal.

What about those times when we have each stated fully our ideas and yet we cannot agree on a course of action? I suggest that if the decision can wait (and most of them can), then wait. While you are waiting, you and your spouse should be praying and seeking new information that may shed light on the situation. A week later, discuss it again and see where you are.

"How long do we wait?" As long as you can! In my opinion, the only time that a husband should make a decision without mutual agreement is on those rare occasions when the decision must be made "today." There are few such decisions in life. Most things can wait. Unity is more important than haste. "But if I don't buy it today, the sale will be over!" A "bargain" at the expense of unity with your mate is costly indeed.

On those occasions when the decision must be made "today" and there is still no agreement between partners, I believe the husband has the responsibility to make the decision that he feels is best. He must also bear full responsibility for that decision.

At this point, the wife may feel the challenge of submission, but she should also feel the security of a responsible husband, one who will make decisions when he must. In such decisions, the wife should not feel responsible for the husband's choice. On the other hand, neither should she work for its failure.

If, indeed, time reveals that it was a poor decision, the wife should never yield to the temptation to say, "I told you so. If you had listened to me, this would not have happened." When a man is down, he does not need someone to step on him. He needs a gentle arm and soft assurance that you are with him and that things will work out. "We goofed, but we're together, and we'll make it." These are the words of the wise wife.

Just as God the Father is always looking out for the interests of God the Son, so the husband is to be looking out for the interests of his wife. The husband who has this mindset will never purposely make decisions that will be harmful. Rather, he is asking how this decision will affect her and is seeking to make decisions that will enhance her life as well as their relationship.

Josh was a husband who had learned to make decisions based on love for his wife. "I want to tell you the hardest decision I ever made in my life and one of the best decisions I've ever made," he said during a break at a marriage seminar I was leading in Washington, DC. He explained he had been in the military fifteen years when he had a growing desire to start a business as a civilian. He talked with his wife about it, and she suggested that Josh explore more fully what their lifestyle would be if he started a business.

"So I contacted a man who was in a similar business and spent a day talking with him about his own vocational journey. I discovered that in the early years of starting the business, he had almost lost his wife because of the time and energy involved in his business. I reasoned that that would never happen to me because of my commitment to Candice.

"I discussed all of this with her, and as time went on, she had a growing uneasiness about our leaving the military. I had five years until full retirement and Candice genuinely liked the military lifestyle. It had also been good for our children.

"The more we talked, the more I began to realize that getting out of the military at this point was probably not a sign of wisdom. But I was so eager to start my business. I prayed and prayed, but it seemed like I couldn't get any direction from God. Then one day, I heard a preacher make this comment: 'God gave us a lot of guidance when He gave us wives.'

"It was like the voice of God to me. I realized that Candice was giving me genuine wisdom and that it was my selfish ambitions that were pulling me in the other direction. So I made the decision to stay in the military. I'm sure it was one of the best decisions I've ever made.

"It's been seven years since I finished the twenty years and decided to continue. I've now been in the military twenty-seven years and my plans are to make it thirty. God has given us a wonderful ministry with military couples. We know that marriages are under great stress and our passion has been to help military couples have strong marriages. I know that we would not have had this ministry if I had gone into business. I thank God every day for giving me guidance through Candice."

Josh discovered the biblical principle that "two are better than one" and that often God uses our spouse to give us wisdom.

I am well aware that some will reject the idea that the husband should be the leader in decision making. However, when one understands the biblical pattern of such leadership, it becomes more feasible. Male leadership in the home has nothing to do with superiority. It has to do with order among equals. Sooner or later, if one partner is not recognized as the leader, the couple will come to a stale-mate and will be rendered ineffective when a crisis comes. We must strive for unity in all de-cisions, and with proper attitudes such will be attained 95 percent of the time—but someone must have the responsibility for making deci-sions when unity cannot be achieved.

> *Many couples need to be reminded that they are on the same team.*

Many couples need to be reminded that they are on the same team. Too often, partners are competing with each other, each defending his/her own ideas. Nothing could be more foolish. Share your ideas, by all means, but use those ideas to come to the best decision. Not my ideas versus your ideas, but our ideas and our decision. "We feel; we think; we decided." This is the language of unity.

At the risk of sounding redundant, let me note carefully what the Scrip-ture does not mean when it says, "The husband is the head of his wife" (Ephe-sians 5:23).

The statement does not mean that the husband is more intelligent than the wife. Certainly, a given husband might have a higher IQ than his wife or a given wife a higher IQ than her husband, but headship has nothing to do with intelligence. God the Father and God the Son are equally infinite in wisdom, yet the Father is the "head" of the Son. Generally speaking, men and women are both highly intelligent creatures (though one may wonder about that at times).

IN GOD'S IMAGE

"The husband is the head of his wife" does not mean that the man is more valuable than the woman. Both men and women are made in the image of God and are of infinite worth. It is true that the Old Testament records the Jewish system, which exalted the male child as more valuable than the female, but we must not accept the Jewish cultural system as God's system. The angels in heaven do not rejoice more when a man is converted than when a woman is converted. In Christ "there is no longer . . . male and female"; they "are all one" (Galatians 3:28).

"The husband is the head of his wife" does not mean that the husband is to be a dictator, making independent decisions and telling his wife what to do. We certainly do not see that pattern between God the Father and God the Son. It is unthinkable that God the Father would make a decision and then call in the Son and inform Him. "The Lord our God, the Lord is one" (Deuteronomy 6:4 NIV). There is full and complete communication and absolute unity in every decision.

Many a Christian dictator has brought ulcers upon himself by carrying an inordinate load of responsibility. God did not intend the husband to make all the decisions alone. Remember, the wife was given to be a helper. How can she help when her husband does not even consult her? The great need of our day is for Christian leaders, not dictators.

Many wives shudder when they hear the pastor say, "Turn in your Bible to Ephesians 5:22." They can feel it coming, and they do not like the sound of it. "For wives, this means submit to your husbands as to the Lord."

"But you don't know my husband," they think. "But you don't understand submission," God must say.

In this section, I want to allay some fears by discussing what submission does not mean. Submission does not mean that the wife must do all the "giving." The verse that immediately precedes Ephesians 5:22 reads, "Submit to one another out of reverence for Christ." Submission is a mutual exercise. Neither husbands nor wives can have their own way and a successful marriage at the same time. That is why God instructs husbands to love their wives "as Christ loved the church" (Ephesians 5:25). The word translated "love" here indicates a self-giving love that seeks the benefit of the one loved.

For example, a husband may well submit to attending a party that he has no personal desire to attend in order to enhance the marriage. Likewise, a wife may submit to attending a football game about which she understands little in order to share one of her husband's joys. Submission is the opposite of demanding one's own way and is required on the part of both husband and wife.

Submission does not mean that the wife cannot express her ideas. Why would God give a wife the capacity for ideas if she were not to express them? You are called to be a helper. How can you help when you refuse to share your wisdom?

"But my husband is not open to my ideas." That is his problem, not yours. Silence is never the road to unity. You may need to develop tact and exercise wisdom as to the time and manner in which you express yourself, but you must utilize the mind that God has given you. You have a responsibility. You cannot stand idly by and watch your husband fail. You must seek to be a constructive helper.

Finally, submission does not mean that the wife makes no decisions. We have talked mainly about major decisions in the home, and we have said that the basic pattern is mutual expression of ideas with a view to unity under the leadership of the husband. In the average home, however, there will be entire areas in which the couple agrees that the wife will make the decisions.

FINDING UNITY THROUGH OUR DIFFERENCES

David and Brenda from Spokane, Washington, gave me a good example of this decision-making pattern. Brenda's college major was journalism. She was an avid reader and had kept a daily journal since her college days. She was working for a local newspaper until her first child was born, at which time she decided to be a stay-at-home mom, although she continued to write articles for the paper from time to time. David worked for an advertising agency. He was strong on creativity and weak on organization.

After numerous conflicts in their marriage, which typically ended in arguments, David was in church one Sunday and heard a sermon on spiritual gifts.

The idea was that God has given each Christian special abilities and that His design is that each person will use those gifts for the good of the larger community. The pastor was talking about using these gifts in the context of the local church, but David applied the concept to his marriage:

"It was like I had made a great discovery that Brenda was designed to do certain things well and I was designed to do other things well. And that God had placed us together so that we could work as an efficient team. In the past, I had been trying to 'run the show' rather than utilizing each of our strengths. Brenda and I talked about all of this on that Sunday afternoon and made some significant decisions together. We agreed that in certain areas of our lives, she would make all of the decisions and would consult me only if she desired my input. In other areas, I would make the decisions. We also agreed that either of us could ask questions of the other but that, in those areas, we would trust the other person to make the final decision.

"It was one of the best things we have ever done. It removed the tension between the two of us when we saw ourselves as partners, working together to build a strong marriage, utilizing our strengths."

Many couples have found this pattern of decision making workable. It makes the most of our differences and emphasizes our unity. Of course, this could be carried to the extreme. Perhaps you've heard of the husband who said, "In the very beginning of our marriage, we agreed that I would make all of the major decisions and my wife would make the decisions that related to day-to-day activities. We've been married twenty-five years and so far, there haven't been any major decisions."

It would be poor stewardship of time if both partners gave attention to every detail of life. The sign of wisdom is to agree upon areas of responsibility in which the wife will make decisions at her own discretion. (Of course, she should feel free to ask her husband's advice as she desires.) The areas of her responsibility will vary from family to family but may involve food, clothing, home decorating, automobiles, education, areas of child rearing, and so on.

Proverbs 31:10–31, the description of a godly woman, contains a tremendous range of decision making that was committed to the wife. She certainly could not have felt that her abilities were not being utilized. I suggest that the wise and mature couple will share responsibilities based on their individual interests and abilities. A husband who is secure in his own self-esteem will not view his wife's efforts as competition. A wife who recognizes her own God-given self-worth will not have to prove her worth to anyone. A husband and a wife who work as a team, each encouraging the other to reach his/her maximum potential for God, will both find the rewards satisfying.

IN CLOSING

In summary, I am suggesting that if a couple will agree on a pattern for decision making, they can avoid many battles. The biblical pattern I am suggesting is that of mutual and complete expression of ideas and feelings relating to the questions at hand, seeking to come to a unanimous decision—one that both agree is the best decision.

When such a consensus cannot be reached, wait and look for further guidance. Discuss the subject again later and seek unity. If indeed you have not reached such unity, and the decision must be made right away, then the husband should make the decision that he feels is best and bear the responsibility for that decision. The wife should admit her disagreement but express willingness to work with her husband and accept his leadership. Such an attitude will eventually bring a unity of heart that is far more important than any particular issue.

Your Turn

1. In one paragraph answer the following question: How are decisions made in our home? (Describe the process as clearly as possible.)

2. If you decided to follow the decision-making pattern discussed in this chapter, what changes would have to be made? Make a list of these changes.

3. Ask your partner to read the chapter and answer the two questions above.

4. When both of you have completed these assignments, agree upon a time to discuss decision making with a view to growth. The following questions may serve as a guide to your discussion:

   • Do we agree that unity between husband and wife is our goal in decision making?

   • What has been our most common problem in reaching unity of decisions?

   • What do we need to change in order to overcome this problem?

   • Have we agreed on who is to make the decision on those rare occasions when the decision must be made "today" and we still do not have unity?

5. Read Philippians 2:2–4. What guidelines does this passage suggest for decision making in the home?

CHAPTER SEVEN

"You Mean We Have to Work at Sex?"

THE MOVIES MAKE it look so easy. Two beautiful bodies, falling into one another's arms, coming together as one . . .

The dreams and hopes of a bride and groom are many, but perhaps none is brighter than the dream of sexual oneness in marriage. Many enter marriage with the vision of one great sex orgy—morning, noon, and night. Obviously, for thousands in our country those dreams are shattered and hopes never realized. Why is it that cultured, educated spouses cannot find satisfaction in this very important area of marriage? Part of the answer lies in unrealistic expectations.

Our society has been unfair to us. Films, magazines, and novels have conveyed the idea that sexual thrill and mutual satisfaction are automatic when two bodies come together. We are told that all that is required for sexual fulfillment is two consenting parties. That is simply not true. Sex is far more intricate and wonderful than that. When we enter marriage with the misconception that fulfillment in this area will "come naturally," we are headed for disappointment.

Even couples who have been sexually active with each other before marriage will not automatically find mutual sexual fulfillment.

Sexual oneness, by which I mean the mutual satisfaction of partners, both enjoying their sexuality and a wholesome sense of sexual fulfillment, does not come automatically. It requires the same degree of commitment and effort as does intellectual oneness or social oneness, which we discussed earlier. Even couples who have been sexually active with each other before marriage will not automatically find mutual sexual fulfillment. Often attitudes and emotions surface after marriage that lay dormant while dating.

Someone will say, "You mean we have to work at sex? I thought that came naturally!" I would reply, "It is that very misconception that will be your greatest barrier to sexual oneness." I am not saying that the sexual aspect of marriage is drudgery, something that requires hard, unrewarding labor. What I am saying is that the time and work invested in this area will pay you back many times over.

Those couples who grow toward maturity in this area will be the recipients of a smile from the Creator, who said, "And the two are united into one" (Genesis 2:24). Those who do not obtain sexual oneness will never know the joy of total marriage. Anything less than a deep sense of fulfillment on the part of both partners is something less than what is available. What, then, are the guidelines that will lead us to such oneness?

A HEALTHY ATTITUDE

One of the barriers to sexual oneness is a negative attitude toward sex in general and intercourse in particular. Such attitudes may have their origin in a poor parental example, a distorted sex education, an unfortunate sexual experience as a child, or sexual involvement as a teenager that brought disappointment and guilt. The origin is relatively unimportant. The important thing is to understand that we are masters of our attitudes. We do not need to be a slave to our negative feelings forever.

The first step in overcoming such negative attitudes is an exposure to the truth. Jesus said, "If you remain faithful to my teachings . . . you will know the truth, and the truth will set you free" (John 8:31–32). What is the truth about sex?

The truth is that sex is God's idea. As we discussed earlier, it was God who made us male and female. Humanity has exploited sex, but humanity did not originate sex. A holy God, totally separate from sin, made us sexual beings. Therefore, sex is wholesome and good.

Our maleness and femaleness is a righteous idea. There is nothing dirty about our sexual organs. They are exactly as God intended them to be. He is a perfect Creator, and all that He has made is good. We must not relinquish the sanctity of sex because people have exploited and cheapened it by misuse. Sex is not the trademark of the world; it bears the personal label "made by God."

Sometimes even the church has been guilty of distorting this truth. In our eagerness to condemn the misuse of sex, we have conveyed the idea that sex itself is evil. Such is not the case. Paul wrote, "[Our bodies] were made for the Lord . . . your body is the temple of the Holy Spirit" (1 Corinthians 6:13, 19). All of our body is good and clean.

The second step in overcoming a negative attitude toward sex is to respond to the truth. If, indeed, sex is a gift of God and sexual intercourse between husband and wife is God's desire for us, then I must not allow my distorted emotions to keep me from God's will. I must admit my feelings to God and to my mate and then thank God that I do not have to follow those feelings. Such a prayer might even be prayed audibly during the sex act itself. As I do God's will in fellowship with Him, my emotions and attitudes will change. If I foster these negative emotions by refusing to become involved in an expression of love through intercourse with my mate, I am failing to exercise my freedom to live above my emotions. Positive actions must precede positive emotions.

OVERCOMING PAST EXPERIENCES

One of the realities of contemporary society is that many couples come to marriage with previous sexual experience, either with each other or other partners—and this is just as true among our Christian young people as it is among secular youth, according to longtime evangelical observer Ronald J. Sider in his essay, "The Scandal of the Evangelical Conscience."[1]

Clearly, many couples, particularly in the early years of marriage, need to deal with the baggage of past sexual experience. The commonly held idea is that sexual experience before marriage better prepares you for marriage. Research indicates otherwise.[2] In fact, the divorce rate among those who have had previous sexual experience is higher than those who have had no sexual experience before marriage. The reality is that previous sexual experience often becomes a psychological barrier in achieving sexual oneness in marriage.

The Christian answer to such barriers is the confession of wrongdoing and genuinely forgiving each other for past failures. The scars of the past may remain forever, but scars can serve as reminders of the grace and love of God. One area in which the scars are most troublesome is when one partner has contracted a sexually transmitted disease before marriage. Most of these diseases are treatable but not curable. These are scars with which the couple must live and to which they must adjust. A more serious problem is when the sexually transmitted disease existed before marriage, but was not communicated to the spouse. This is, in essence, a deception and often becomes a source of intense tension between the couple and has at times led to an early divorce. In my premarital counseling, I always encourage couples to tell the truth about past experiences. If these cannot be worked through in the dating context, they will be far more difficult after marriage. If, however, we go into marriage with our eyes open to the past and are willing to accept the person as he or she is, then we are far more likely to process the problems after marriage.

"HOW COULD I HELP YOU?"

If there is one word that is more important in gaining sexual oneness than any other, it is the word *communication*. Why are we so ready to discuss everything else and so reticent to communicate openly about this area of our lives? Your wife can never know your feelings, needs, and desires if you do not express them. Your husband will never know what pleases you if you do not communicate. I have never heard of a couple who gained sexual oneness without open communication about sexual matters.

A wife once stated in my office that she had been married for three years and had never had a sexual orgasm. She had never communicated this to her husband, however. She did not want to hurt him. Perhaps there was something wrong with her, she reasoned. She had inquired of her doctor and was assured that there was no physical problem. When she finally told all this to her husband, the problem was soon solved. A husband cannot work on a problem about which he is unaware. A husband, however, ought to be asking questions to determine the satisfaction of his wife.

In an attempt to foster communication in my family-life seminars, I have periodically asked wives and husbands to write out the advice they would like to give their mates regarding the sex act. That is, "What suggestions would you make to your mate that you feel would make the sexual act more meaningful?" A collection of these suggestions is to be found at the end of this chapter. It is hoped that they will encourage you and your partner to renew communication in this area.

WHY SEX?

Some couples have difficulty in growth because they do not understand the purpose of sex as revealed in Scripture. The most obvious purpose, but certainly not the only purpose, is that of procreation. Having created man, male and female, "God blessed them and said, 'Be fruitful and multiply. Fill the earth'" (Genesis 1:28). Sexual intercourse for the purpose of procreation is God's way of letting us share in the thrill of creation. There are few human thrills to equal that of looking into the face of a baby, the offspring of your love for your mate.

Children are always viewed in Scripture as the gift of God. "Children are a gift from the Lord; they are a reward from him" (Psalm 127:3). What, then, of contraception? Some would argue that the original command of God to "fill the earth" has now been accomplished—at least in poorer countries struggling with overpopulation. Therefore, we must stop "filling" the earth, lest we overflow the earth.

There is, however, a higher principle involved. We are created responsible creatures. Throughout Scripture, parents are viewed as responsible for caring for the needs of children whom they "create." As a responsible parent, I must use reason in deciding how many children I can care for realistically. As God has given us medical help through the effort of dedicated men and women, so He has given us means of limiting births. It is interesting that such knowledge has come in the generations of greatest need as far as overpopulation is concerned. As Christians, we are to use all God's gifts in a responsible manner. Therefore, I believe that a couple should discuss and decide together when they will use birth control and what method of birth control they will use as responsible persons. This matter should be discussed with the doctor when the couple goes for premarital examinations.

The second purpose of sexual intercourse within marriage revealed in the Bible is to meet physical and emotional needs. Paul speaks to this point when he says:

> The husband should fulfill his wife's sexual needs, and the wife should fulfill her husband's needs. The wife gives authority over her body to her husband, and the husband gives authority over his body to his wife. Do not deprive each other of sexual relations, unless you both agree to refrain from sexual intimacy for a limited time so you can give yourselves more completely to prayer. Afterward, you should come

together again so that Satan won't be able to tempt you because of your lack of self-control. (1 Corinthians 7:3–5)

Paul is dealing with the reality of the strong physical/emotional need that the husband and wife have for each other. We are sexual beings, and we do have this strong desire for each other sexually. Indeed, our greatest problem before marriage is controlling this strong desire. But within marriage, that desire is to find full satisfaction in sexual intercourse.

When we refuse each other this privilege, we frustrate the expressed pattern that God has revealed. If, indeed, husbands and wives would take this responsibility seriously, the rate of extramarital affairs would be drastically lowered.

An honest wife will say, "But I don't feel like having intercourse as often as my husband desires." Openly and honestly express your feelings to your mate, but also let him know that you stand ready to meet his needs. You need not go through all the foreplay and energy-consuming activity if you are fatigued. Simply let him know that you love him and want to meet his needs. This can normally be done very shortly with a minimum of energy. The wife should not be forced to have an orgasm if she does not desire such. If needs are met, then one of the purposes of sex is accomplished.

A third purpose of sex revealed in Scripture is to *provide pleasure*. Those who feel that God wished to make life as miserable as possible for His subjects may have difficulty with this one. But Scripture makes clear that God's plans for us are always good: "'For I know the plans I have for you,' says the Lord. 'They are plans for good and not for disaster, to give you a future and a hope'" (Jeremiah 29:11). God did not have to make the sexual act pleasurable, but He did. It is one of those above-and-beyond acts for which God is noted.

"PLEASURE" IN THE BIBLE

The eighteenth chapter of Genesis records a very interesting event in the life of Abraham and Sarah. The messenger of God had come to proclaim that they were to have a son. A wonderful idea, but Abraham was one hundred years old, and Sarah was ninety! Abraham posed a reasonable question to this heavenly messenger, and the Scriptures say that in response Sarah "laughed silently to herself and said, 'How could a worn-out woman like me enjoy such pleasure, especially when my master—my husband—is also so old?'" (Genesis 18:12). The word translated "pleasure" is not the normal Hebrew word for pleasure and is used only here in the Old Testament. Sarah is reflecting upon the pleasurable experience of the sex act. She is old. The body chemistry is not what it used to be, but she is not too old to remember that it was a pleasurable experience.

The Song of Solomon is replete with illustrations of the pleasure of the sexual aspect of marriage (6:1–9; 7:1–10). The descriptive phrases may be foreign to our culture, but the intent is clear. Maleness and femaleness are meant to be enjoyed by marriage partners.

Another intriguing passage is found in Deuteronomy 24:5, where we are told, "A newly married man must not be drafted into the army or be given any other official responsibilities. He must be free to spend one year at home, bringing happiness to the wife he has married." The word translated "happiness" is elsewhere translated "pleasure" and is the same word that is used for sexual gratification. He is to stay home and "pleasure" his wife for one year. Talk about a honeymoon!

EXPRESSING LOVE DURING THE HONEYMOON . . . AND AFTER

This is a good place to digress for a moment and say a word about the honeymoon. We try to crowd it into three days or a week at most. It is supposed to be heaven on earth, but for many it is a very disappointing time. If God suggested a year for pleasure, what makes us think we can have sexual paradise in three days? Let me reiterate that sexual oneness takes time.

The typical American honeymoon is a very pressured time. For weeks you have expended your energy in preparation for the wedding. The bachelor parties and showers are now over. The last handful of confetti has rained upon your heads, and now you are alone. Physical and emotional exhaustion are not the companions of a meaningful sexual experience. Sexual adjustment is begun with two strikes against you.

"I remember we were exhausted," one woman said. "We were in one of the finest hotels in downtown Chicago, in a lovely, spacious room. We just sat by the window for a time in a semidaze, looking out at the traffic on Lake Shore Drive and admiring a huge complimentary fruit bowl on the coffee table. Finally it was time for bed. And . . . it was fine, but we realized we were both desperately in need of a good night's sleep."

Do not expect too much from your honeymoon. At best, it is the mere beginning of what is to come. Your sexual enjoyment on the honeymoon will be minimal compared to that of a year later if you commit yourselves to growth in oneness.

Very closely related to the idea of pleasure is the concept of love. One of the desires of love is to give pleasure to the one loved. Therefore, sexual intercourse within marriage becomes a very meaningful method of expressing love. It is one of love's loudest voices. This means that each mate must think of the other's pleasure (Philippians 2:3–4). The husband is to "pleasure" his wife, and the wife is to "pleasure" her husband. It is in mutual self-giving that love finds its highest expression.

HIS AND HER NEEDS—THEY DIFFER!

"Look at you!" exclaims the husband admiringly as he and his wife get dressed in the morning. "How could he even *think* about this now?" she wonders to herself as she rummages for her good black pants. The answer: physiology. And psychology. We've all heard a lot about the differences between women and men in recent years, but a refresher course is helpful—and will enhance oneness.

It should be noted, for example, that for the male the sex drive is more physically based than for the female. That is, the male gonads are continually producing sperm cells. These cells, along with seminal fluid, are stored in the seminal vesicles. When the seminal vesicles are full, there is a physical demand for release. There is nothing comparable to this in the female.

For the female, the sexual need is more emotional than physical. The implications of this difference are readily observed. For example, the husband would experience little difficulty in having sexual intercourse one hour after a "knockdown-drag-out" argument with his wife. The wife, on the other hand, would find this almost impossible. Her emotions are too involved. She cannot have meaningful sexual fulfillment when things are not right in other areas of the relationship.

The suggestions on the following pages will show that for the wife good sexual relations begin in the morning and are enhanced with all those little positive expressions of thoughtfulness on the part of the husband throughout the day. Kindness and thoughtfulness on the part of the husband pave the way for meaningful sexual experiences.

We need to understand the differences in the physical-emotional responses of males and females in the act of sexual intercourse itself. The husband tends to come to an emotional-physical climax rather rapidly, and after the climax his emotions drop rapidly, whereas the wife is much more gradual in her emotional changes, both before and after climax. This difference has many implications for the husband and wife who wish to experience physical oneness (as the suggestions on the following pages indicate).

It is beyond the purpose of this volume to deal with all the details of sexual adjustment. Excellent materials are available (see Resources), and I highly recommend the following for additional resource information: *The Gift of Sex* by Clifford and Joyce Penner, and *Sheet Music* by Kevin Leman.

In addition, I recommend another book by the Penners, *The Married Guy's Guide to Great Sex*. They are outstanding Christian counselors, and this book is written to help husbands who want to experience God's best in physical oneness.

All these resources are excellent and give practical help in sexual adjustment. They should be in the lending library of every Christian couple.

IN CLOSING

Some may wish life were like Hollywood, where beautiful stars with perfect bodies mate on-screen with total passion and no problems. God, however, in His infinite wisdom, gave us His gift of sex to create children, to provide pleasure, and to bring husband and wife closer together in the intimate bond of marriage. He intends the two of you to spend a lifetime exploring one another physically, spiritually, intellectually, and emotionally. That does not mean there will be no adjustment or no challenges! But because it is God's best for you, the journey toward intimacy is well worth the commitment.

Your Turn

1. How would you rate the sexual aspect of your marriage?

   ____ excellent   ____ good   ____ fair   ____ poor

2. In a short paragraph, write your attitude toward the sexual aspect of marriage.

3. If you are a wife, read "Suggestions Wives Have Made to Husbands: How to Make Sexual Relations More Meaningful." Check those items you would like to mention to your husband.

4. If you are a husband, read "Suggestions Husbands Have Made to Wives: How to Make Sexual Relations More Meaningful." Check those items you would like to mention to your wife.

5. When both of you are feeling good and are open to growth, discuss with each other the items you have checked. Concentrate on what your partner is saying, rather than on trying to defend yourself. The purpose of conversation is growth, not defense.

6. At another time, write down for yourself what you can and will do to grow in physical oneness with your mate. A month from now, check your list to see what improvements you have made. Set new goals each month.

SUGGESTIONS HUSBANDS HAVE MADE TO WIVES:

How to Make Sexual Relations More Meaningful

1. Be aggressive occasionally.
2. Be innovative and imaginative.
3. Do not be ashamed to show that you are enjoying it.
4. Be attractive at bedtime. Wear something besides "granny" gowns and everyday pajamas.
5. Do things to catch my attention; men are easily excited by sight.
6. Communicate more openly about sex; communicate readiness for the actual act once foreplay has excited sufficiently.
7. Go to bed earlier.
8. Do not make me feel guilty at night for my inconsistencies during the day (not being affectionate enough, and so on).
9. Prolong the sexual relationship at times.
10. Be more aware of my needs and desires as a man.
11. Participate more fully and freely in the sexual act; be more submissive and open.
12. Allow variety in the time for the sexual act (not always at night).
13. Show more desire, and understand that caressing and foreplay are as important to me as they are to you.
14. Do not allow yourself to remain upset over everyday events that go wrong.
15. Relax together at least once a week.
16. Do not always play "hard to get."
17. Clear your mind of daily things (today's and tomorrow's) and think about the matter at hand—love.
18. Do not try to fake enjoyment.
19. Do not try to punish me by denying me sex or by giving it grudgingly.
20. Treat me like your lover.

Suggestions Wives Have Made to Husbands:
How to Make Sexual Relations More Meaningful

1. Show more affection and attention throughout the day; come in after work and kiss my neck.

2. Spend more time in foreplay; love, play, and romantic remarks are important.

3. Encourage the sex act at various times, rather than always at night when we're tired.

4. Be more sympathetic when I am really sick.

5. Be the aggressive one instead of waiting for me to make the first move.

6. Accept me as I am; accept me even when you see the worst side of me.

7. Tell me that you love me at times other than when we are in bed; phone sometimes just to say "I love you!" Do not be ashamed to say "I love you" in front of others.

8. While I am showering, find soft music on the radio.

9. Honor Christ as the Head of the home.

10. Be sweet and loving at least one hour before initiating sex.

11. Help me to feel I am sexually and romantically attractive by complimenting me often.

12. Tell me what you enjoy and when you are excited; express your desires more openly; share yourself more fully with me.

13. Try not to ejaculate so soon.

14. Pray with me about the problems and victories you are having; let me express my own needs to you.

15. Appreciate the beauty of nature and share this appreciation with me.

16. Take more of the responsibility for getting the children settled so that I can relax and share more of the evening with you.

17. Be patient with me; do not ridicule my slowness to reach orgasm.

18. Do not approach lovemaking as a ritualistic activity; make each time a new experience. Do not let lovemaking get boring by doing the same things over and over; try new things or new places.

19. Never try to make love with me when you are harboring negative feelings toward me or you know things are not right; let there be harmony between us so that sexual intercourse can indeed be an act of love.

20. Think of something nice to say about me in front of others occasionally.

CHAPTER EIGHT

Leaving and Honoring Parents

I REMEMBER ONCE I had a conversation with my father-in-law before I got married," a husband said. "He said something like, 'Give her a good life. Take care of her.' He wasn't big on advice, and he's gone now, but that's always stuck with me, like I have a trust."

"When I was first married my mother-in-law really irritated me," said this man's wife. "I complained a lot to my husband, who to his credit was supportive of me. At the same time, I saw how close he and his mom were and realized I didn't want to undermine that. As she grew elderly I began to think about what it means to 'honor' your parents and in-laws. That's a command, not an option . . . and now that she's gone, I try to honor her memory and share funny stories about her with my husband." For better and sometimes for worse, our parents and parents-in-law are intimately, inextricably part of our lives. But whether we're newlyweds or an "old married couple," *how* should they be a part of our lives?

We need one another. A newly married couple needs the emotional warmth and life wisdom that comes from a healthy relationship with both sets of parents, and parents need the emotional warmth and companionship (and, perhaps, grandchildren!) that comes from the couple. Life is too short to live with broken relationships. If there are conflicts in the relationship, the principle of confession and forgiveness discussed in chapter 2 applies to in-laws as well as to marriage partners. We do not have to agree with each other in order to have a wholesome relationship, but bitterness and resentment are always wrong (Ephesians 4:31). Mutual freedom and mutual respect should be the guiding principle for parents and their married children.

What guidelines does the Bible give for in-law relationships? How should the married couple respond to parents' ideas, suggestions, and needs? What can we do when we see parents destroying our marital unity? Two principles must be kept in balance if we are to follow the biblical patterns in our relationships with in-laws: new allegiance and continued honor.

"LEAVING" PARENTS

In Genesis 2:24 we read, "This explains why a man leaves his father and mother and is joined to his wife, and the two are united into one." This principle is repeated in Ephesians 5:31. God's pattern for marriage involves the "leaving" of parents and the "cleaving" to one's mate. Marriage involves a change of allegiance. Before marriage, one's allegiance is to one's parents, but after marriage allegiance shifts to one's mate.

It is what the psychologists call "cutting the psychological apron strings." No longer does the individual lean on his parents but rather on his mate. If there is a conflict of interest between a man's wife and his mother, the husband is to stand with his wife. This does not mean that the mother is to be treated unkindly. That is the second principle, which we will deal with shortly. The principle of separating from parents is, however, extremely important. No couple will reach their full potential in marriage without this psychological break from parents.

What does this principle mean in the practical realm? I believe that it suggests separate living arrangements for the newly married couple. While living with parents, the couple cannot develop independence as readily as when living alone. The dependency on parents is enhanced as long as they live with parents. Living in a meager apartment with the freedom to develop their own lifestyle under God is better than luxurious living in the shadow of parents. Parents should encourage such independence, and the ability to provide such living accommodations should be a factor in setting the wedding date.

The principle of "leaving" parents is also important in decision making. Your parents may have suggestions about many aspects of your married life. Each suggestion should be taken seriously, but, in the final analysis, you must make your own decision. You should no longer make decisions on the basis of what would make parents happy but on the basis of what would make your partner happy. Under God, you are a new unit, brought together by His Spirit to live for each other (Philippians 2:3–4).

This means that the time may come when a husband must sit down with his mother and say, "Mom, you know that I love you very much, but you also know that I am now married. I cannot break up my marriage in order to do what you desire. I love you, and I want to help you, but I must do what I believe is right for my wife and me. I hope you understand because I want to continue the warm relationship that we have had through the years. But if you do not understand, then that is a problem you must work through. I must give myself to the building of my marriage."

If such a statement sounds harsh to you, be thankful. It is because you have not encountered a stubborn, selfish, carnal mother-in-law. Such do exist, and firmness with love is the biblical answer to correcting the situation. A husband must not allow his mother to continue to control his life after marriage. Such is not the biblical pattern.

CONSIDERING PARENTS' WISDOM

On the other hand, parents' suggestions should be given due consideration. Our parents are older and perhaps wiser. A good example of the wisdom of a father-in-law is found in Exodus 18. Moses was working from morning till evening judging the people of Israel. The waiting room was always filled, and there was no time for coffee breaks. "'This is not good!' Moses' father-in-law exclaimed. 'You're going to wear yourself out—and the people, too. This job is too heavy a burden for you to handle all by yourself. Now listen to me, and let me give you a word of advice, and may God be with you. You should continue to be the people's representative before God, bringing their disputes to him'" (vv. 17–19).

He went on to suggest that the crowds be divided into thousands, hundreds, fifties, and tens, and that authority be delegated to other qualified men who would judge those under their jurisdiction. Moses then would be free to spend more time with God and in teaching the people the law of God (vv. 19–20). Thus, his would be more of a "preventive" ministry rather than a "crisis" ministry. Only the difficult cases would be brought to him for judgment (v. 22).

Moses saw the wisdom of such a suggestion and adopted it. In so doing, he revealed his own maturity. He did not have to rebel against a good idea just because it came from his father-in-law. He was secure enough in his own self-worth that he could accept a good idea, regardless of its source.

The principle of separation from parents also has implications when conflict arises in marriage. A young wife who has always leaned heavily on her mother will have a tendency to complain to her when problems arise in the marriage. The next day her husband recognizes that he was wrong, asks forgiveness, and harmony is restored. The daughter fails to tell her mother this. The next time a conflict arises she again confides in Mom. This becomes a pattern, and before long, her mother has a bitter attitude toward the son-in-law and is encouraging the daughter to separate from him. The daughter has been very unfair to her husband and has failed to follow the principle of "leaving" parents.

If you have conflicts in your marriage (and most of us do), seek to solve them by direct confrontation with your mate. Conflict should be a stepping-stone to growth. If you find that you need outside help, then go to your pastor or a Christian marriage counselor. They are trained and equipped by God to give practical help. They can be objective and give biblical guidelines. Parents find it almost impossible to be objective.

HONORING PARENTS

The second principle relating to our relationship with parents is found in Exodus 20:12 and is one of the Ten Commandments: "Honor your father and mother. Then you will live a long, full life in the land the Lord your God is giving you." It is repeated in Deuteronomy 5:16 and Ephesians 6:2–3.

> *The command to honor our parents has never been rescinded. As long as they live, it is right to honor them.*

The command to honor our parents has never been rescinded. As long as they live, it is right to honor them. In Ephesians 6:1, the apostle Paul says, "Children, obey your parents because you belong to the Lord, for this is the right thing to do." Obedience to parents is the guideline from birth to marriage. Paul's second statement is, "'Honor your father and mother.' This is the first commandment with a promise: If you honor your father and mother, 'things will go well for you, and you will have a long life on the earth'" (vv. 2–3). Honor to parents is the guideline from birth to death. Honor was the original command and stands forever.

The word *honor* means "to show respect." It involves treating one with kindness and dignity. It is true that not all parents live respectable lives. Their actions may not be worthy of honor, but because they are made in the image of God, they are worthy of honor. You can respect them for their humanity and for their position as your parents, even when you cannot respect their actions. It is always right to honor your parents and those of your marriage partner. "Leaving" parents for the purpose of marriage does not erase the responsibility to honor them.

How is this honor expressed in daily life? You honor them in such practical actions as visiting, calling, emailing photos, and in general sharing life as much as is feasible, depending on the distances between you. You communicate to them that you still love them and want to share life with them. "Leaving" must never be interpreted as "deserting." Regular contact is essential to honoring parents. Failure to communicate with parents is saying, in effect, "I no longer care."

A further word is necessary regarding communication with parents. Equal treatment of both sets of parents must be maintained. Remember, "For God does not show favoritism" (Romans 2:11). We must follow His example. In practice, this means that our emails, texts, calls, and visits must indicate our commitment to the principle of equality. If one set of parents is phoned once a month, then the other set should be phoned once a month. If one receives a letter or email once a week, then the other should receive the same. The couple should also seek to be equitable in visits, dinners, and vacations.

Perhaps the stickiest situations arise around holidays—Thanksgiving and Christmas. The wife's mother wants them home for Christmas Eve. The husband's mother wants them home for Christmas dinner. That may be possible if they live in the same town, but when they are five hundred miles apart, it becomes impossible. The solution must be based on the principle of equality. This may mean Christmas with one set of parents one year and with the other the following year.

To "honor" implies also that we speak kindly with parents and in-laws. Paul admonishes: "Never speak harshly to an older man, but appeal to him respectfully as you would to your own father" (1 Timothy 5:1). We are to be understanding and sympathetic. Certainly we are to speak the truth, but it must always be in love (Ephesians 4:15). The command of Ephesians 4:31–32 must be taken seriously in our relationship with parents: "Get rid of all bitterness, rage, anger, harsh words, slander, as well as all types of evil behavior. Instead, be kind to each other, tenderhearted, forgiving one another, just as God through Christ has forgiven you." A further

I would advise you to accept your in-laws as they are. Do not feel that it is your task to change them.

114

implication of honor to parents is described in 1 Timothy 5:4: "But if [a widow] has children or grandchildren, their first responsibility is to show godliness at home and repay their parents by taking care of them. This is something that pleases God."

When we were young, our parents met our physical needs. As they grow older, we may have to do the same for them. If and when the need arises, we must bear the responsibility of caring for the physical needs of our parents. To fail in this responsibility is to deny our faith in Christ (1 Timothy 5:8). By our actions, we must show our faith in Christ and honor for our parents.

If I could make some other practical suggestions, I would advise you to accept your in-laws as they are. Do not feel that it is your task to change them. If they are not Christians, certainly you will want to pray for them and look for opportunities to present Christ, but do not try to fit them into your mold. You are expecting them to give you independence to develop your own marriage. Give them the same.

Do not criticize your in-laws to your mate. The responsibility of your mate is to honor his parents. When you criticize them, you make it more difficult for him to follow this pattern. When your mate criticizes the weaknesses of his parents, point out their strengths. Accentuate their positive qualities and encourage honor.

The Bible gives some beautiful examples of wholesome relationships between individuals and their in-laws. Moses had such a wholesome relationship with Jethro, his father-in-law, that, when he informed him of God's call to leave Midian and lead the Israelites out of Egypt, Jethro said, "Go in peace" (Exodus 4:18). Later on, after the success of Moses' venture, his father-in-law came to see him.

"So Moses went out to meet his father-in-law. He bowed low and kissed him. They asked about each other's welfare and then went into Moses' tent" (Exodus 18:7). It was on this visit that Jethro gave Moses the advice that we discussed earlier. His openness to his father-in-law's suggestion shows something of the nature of their relationship.

Ruth and Naomi serve as an example of the devotion of a daughter-in-law to her mother-in-law after the death of both husbands. Jesus directed one of His miracles to the mother-in-law of Peter, and she in turn ministered to Jesus (Matthew 8:14–15).

Freedom and harmony are the biblical ideals for in-law relationships. The train of God's will for marriage must run on the parallel tracks of separation *from* parents and devotion *to* parents.

A WORD TO PARENTS . . .

What if you are an in-law reading this? I ask you to recall the scene of your son's or daughter's wedding. It went something like this:

"I now pronounce you husband and wife," declares the pastor. The new couple is radiant, eyes only for each other. Seated in the front of the church, you, the parents, shed a tear—or weep more openly. This is what all your work has led up to. From the moment of their birth until their marriage, you have been training your children for independence.

Indeed, before your children marry you have been training them to be able to stand on their own feet and operate as mature persons under God. You taught them how to cook meals, wash dishes, make beds, buy clothes, save money, and make responsible decisions. You taught them respect for authority and the value of the individual. In short, you and your spouse have sought to bring them to maturity.

Now, at the time of their marriage, your training ends and their independence reaches fruition. It is hoped that you have helped them move from a state of complete dependence on you, when infants, to complete independence as newlyweds. From this point, your spouse and you must view them as adults who will chart their own course for better or for worse. As parents, we must never again impose our will upon them. We must respect them as equals.

What, then, are our roles as in-laws? Parental involvement in the newlyweds' lives has changed since the days when couples often got married right out of high school or during college. The average age at marriage is now the mid- to late twenties. Often the new couple has been living at a distance. Boomer parents, some married, some not, are busy pursuing their own lives and careers and less likely to want to interfere in their grown kids' lives.

Or are they?

Some things do not change. All parents desire that their grown "children" get a good start. With the benefit of experience and, it is to be hoped, some wisdom, we desire to pass on wise counsel—or at least to help our kids avoid making the same mistakes we did.

Certainly parents should feel freedom to give advice to the young couple (though it is always best to wait until advice is requested). Even so, parents should not seek to force their advice on a couple. Give suggestions if they are requested or if you feel you must, but then withdraw and allow the couple freedom to make their own decisions. Most important, do not express resentment if they do not happen to follow your suggestion. Give them the advantage of your wisdom but the freedom to make their own mistakes. This will be as hard to do as it was when your child was younger . . . but it is the only way they can mature and grow.

What about financial help? The cardinal sin of parents is to use financial assistance to coerce the young couple into conforming to the parents' wishes: "We will buy you a bedroom suite if you move into the house next door." Gifts are fine if they are given out of love without strings attached, but gifts that are conditional become tools rather than gifts. Parents must diligently guard against such temptation.

This does not mean that we will no longer help them, but it means that all help must be given in a responsible manner that will enhance independence, rather than dependence. That is, if we give financial help, it should be with a view toward helping them attain their freedom from our support rather than making them dependent on it. We should not help them establish a lifestyle that they cannot afford to maintain on their own.

IN CLOSING

Many parents and married children find new joy as the family expands. Whether you live around the corner or across the country, you can, too—as God commands and equips.

Your Turn

1. *Do you have any problems with your parents or those of your spouse? If so, write these problems down in specific terms.*

2. *What principles discussed in this chapter have your parents or in-laws violated? Write these down. Be specific. (Read that section again if necessary.)*

3. *Which principles discussed in this chapter have you or your spouse violated with respect to your parents or in-laws? Write these down in specific terms.*

4. *What do you think should be done to correct the situation? Be specific.*

5. *Before discussing your analysis with your spouse, ask him/her to read the section on in-laws in this chapter and complete assignments 1–4 above.*

6. *At an appointed time, have a conference to discuss the problem. Read your statements of the problem to each other and see if:*
   a. you agree on the problem;
   b. you agree on your own failures; and/or
   c. you agree on what actions should be taken to correct the situation.

If not, continue discussion, now or at another time, until you can agree on constructive action.

7. *Having agreed on appropriate action, put your plan into motion. Pray for each other and for your parents and in-laws. (If your plan involves a confrontation with parents, it is usually best for the son or daughter to speak to his/her own parents rather than to in-laws.)*

8. *Be sure that you consider how your own behavior ought to change toward your in-laws and parents. Does your conversation and your behavior indicate that you "honor" them? Be honest. (Respect tends to beget respect.)*

9. *Do all that you do in kindness and firmness. Remember, your desire is to enhance the relationship, not to destroy it.*

CHAPTER NINE

Love and Money

SOMETIMES IT SEEMS as if the more we have, the more we argue about what we have. The poorest of couples in America have abundance compared to the masses of the world's population. I am convinced that the problem does not lie in the amount of money that a couple possesses but in their attitude toward money and the manner in which they handle it.

"I remember years ago when we were struggling financially, we got into a lot of arguments," recalls a wife of my acquaintance. "We were always sitting down to have The Talk about Money, really hash things out, and it invariably wound up in arguing and accusation. We did not like what money issues were doing to us. We finally decided that whatever our circumstance, we would not let it drive us apart and we would stay positive. That has made a huge difference over the years."

DOES "MORE" MEAN "BETTER"?

The author Jeanette Clift George has said, "The great tragedy in life is not in failing to get what you go after. The great tragedy in life is in getting it and finding out it wasn't worth the trouble!"

Most couples assume that if only they made a couple hundred dollars more each month they could meet expenses. But real satisfaction is not found in money (any amount of it) but in "righteousness, godliness, faith, love, endurance and gentleness"—in short, living with God and according to His values (1 Timothy 6:11 NIV). Doing right, responding to others as God would respond, expressing love, being patient with imperfection, and having a realistic appraisal of yourself—these are the things that bring true fulfillment to a marriage.

Once I visited two contrasting homes. The first was a little three-bedroom house. I walked into the living room to find a one-burner oil stove in the center. The baby in its bassinet was in one corner, the dog in another. The walls had only one picture, which accompanied a calendar. Two straight-backed wooden chairs and an ancient couch rested on a rough wooden floor. The doors that led to the kitchen on the left and the bedroom on the right were of the old handmade slat variety with the Z-frame and cracks between each slat.

It was a meager scene by contemporary American standards, but the emotional warmth that I felt as I visited with the young couple was astounding. It was apparent that they loved each other, loved their baby, and loved God. They were happy. Life was exciting.

From there, I crossed to the other side of town and drove up a concrete drive to a beautiful, spacious, brick home. My feet sank into the carpet when I stepped inside. I saw beautiful portraits on the wall as I entered the living room. The fire in the fireplace had an inviting warmth (though the function was aesthetic), and the dog lay on the ultramodern couch.

I sat down to visit, but I had not been there long when I realized that about the only warmth in the family was in the fireplace. I sensed coldness and hostility wrapped in wealth. I drove home that night, saying, "O God, if ever I must choose between those two, give me the three-room house with the emotional warmth of wife and family."

I don't want to romanticize poverty. Studies have shown that constant deprivation and struggle have far-reaching effects on the brain and the emotions. And certainly there are many affluent couples who are true servants of God. But we are to put these things in perspective, as Jesus reminds us: "Seek the Kingdom of God above all else, and live righteously, and he will give you everything you need" (Matthew 6:33). "These things" include food, clothing, and shelter (v. 25). Preoccupation with money—either having it or not having it—can distort our relationship with God and with each other.

Most of us have to work for a living, and it is by this act that God normally provides our necessities. But work is only one "righteous" act. There are many more, such as godliness, faith, love, patience, and meekness. We must not allow the pursuit of money to erode these more important areas, lest we miss life and find money useless.

Jesus warned against this danger when He said, "No one can serve two masters. For you will hate one and love the other; you will be devoted to one and despise the other. You cannot serve both God and money" (Matthew 6:24). Money is an excellent servant, but a poor master; a useful means, but an empty end. When money becomes our god, we are bankrupt indeed.

USING WHAT GOD GIVES US

God cares about how we use what He gives us (Matthew 25:14–30). The Lord said to the faithful steward, "Well done, my good and faithful servant. You have been faithful in handling this small amount, so now I will give you many more responsibilities" (v. 21). "When someone has been given much, much will be required in return" (Luke 12:48).

Financial resources, whether abundant or modest, have tremendous potential for good. As stewards, we are responsible to use in the very best manner all that is entrusted to us. Sound planning, buying, saving, investing, and giving are all part of our stewardship. One aspect of faithful stewardship is giving to God through the church and other Christian organizations. The pattern for giving established in the Old Testament and commended in the New Testament is that of tithing, that is, giving one-tenth of one's income to the direct work of the Lord (Leviticus 27:30; Matthew 23:23).

But more important than amount or percentage is our attitude toward giving. The Scriptures indicate that our giving is to be done with a willing heart. Christian giving is an act of the will prompted by love to God, not a legalistic duty to be performed for merit. Paul speaks to this issue:

> Remember this—a farmer who plants only a few seeds will get a small crop. But the one who plants generously will get a generous crop. You must each decide in your heart how much to give. And don't give reluctantly or in response to pressure. "For God loves a person who gives cheerfully." And God will generously provide all you need. Then you will always have everything you need and plenty left over to share with others. (2 Corinthians 9:6–8)

Many like to claim God's grace and abundance, but they fail to recognize that this promise is made to the cheerful giver. The Scriptures say that one of the purposes of working for wages is that we may be able to give to those who are in need: "If you are a thief, quit stealing. Instead, use your hands for good hard work, and then give generously to others in need" (Ephesians 4:28). Any discussion of finances for the Christian must include provision for regular, proportionate, cheerful giving to the things of God.

YOURS, MINE, AND OURS

As we pursue oneness in marriage, it's important to remember that when we're starting out—and thereafter—it is no longer "my money" and "your money" but rather "our money." In the same manner, it is no longer "my debts" and "your debts" but rather "our debts." If you are to marry a recent graduate who owes $5,000 on an educational loan and you owe $50 on your Visa card, at the conclusion of the wedding ceremony, you are collectively in debt $5,050. When you accept each other as a partner, you accept each other's liabilities as well as each other's assets.

A full disclosure of assets and liabilities should be made before marriage by both partners. It is not wrong to enter marriage with debts, but you ought to know what those debts are, and you ought to agree upon a plan and schedule of repayment. Since they are going to be "our" debts, then "we" need to discuss and agree upon a plan of action.

I have known couples who failed to discuss this area sufficiently before marriage and awakened after the wedding to realize that together they had a debt so large that already they felt a financial noose around their necks. What a tragedy to begin marriage with such a handicap. In my opinion, a large debt without a realistic means of repayment is sufficient cause to postpone the marriage. Financial irresponsibility before marriage is an indicator of financial irresponsibility after marriage. Most couples have some debts when they come to marriage, such as student loans, and a full disclosure by each will allow them to face marriage realistically.

Your assets, too, are now joint assets. She may have $6,000 in a savings account and he may have only $80, but when they choose marriage "they" have $6,080. If you do not feel comfortable with this "oneness," then you are not ready for marriage. Have we not established that the very motif of marriage is oneness? When it comes to finances, you must move toward oneness.

There may be cases where, because of very large estates, the couple may be wise to retain individual ownership of certain properties or assets for tax purposes, but for most of us the principle of oneness implies joint savings accounts, checking accounts, property ownership, and so on. We are one, and so we want to express our oneness in finances as well as in other areas of life.

Since it is "our" money, then "we" ought to agree upon how it will be spent. The pattern for decision making discussed in chapter 6 should apply to financial decisions as well as to other decisions. Full and open discussion should precede any financial decision, and agreement should be the goal of all discussion. Remember, you are partners, not competitors. Marriage is enhanced by agreement in financial matters.

AGREE TO AGREE ON BIG PURCHASES . . . AND A BUDGET

One practical principle that can prevent much tragedy is an agreement on the part of both partners that neither will make a major purchase without consulting the other. The purpose of consulting is to reach agreement regarding the purchase. The term "major purchase" should be clearly defined with a dollar value. For example, the couple might agree that neither would ever buy anything that cost more than fifty dollars without such agreement.

It is true that many flat-screen TVs would still be in the showroom if couples followed this principle, but it is also true that many couples would be far happier. Oneness between marriage partners is more important than any material purchase.

Further, a couple needs to agree upon a pattern for their spending. The word *budget* frightens many couples, but in reality all couples have a budget. A budget is simply a plan for handling money. Many couples do not have a written budget, and many do not have a very effective budget, but all couples have a plan. So the question is not "Should we have a budget?" but rather "How can we improve our budget?" "We already have a plan, but could we have a better plan?"

Budgeting need not be a burdensome bookkeeping procedure of laboriously recording every penny spent. Rather, a budget is a financial plan—simply an application of reason and willpower to the management of your income. You have the choice as to how your money will be spent. It is far better to make that decision based on reason in an open discussion with your mate, than based on emotion when you stand in front of the salesclerk.

PLAN TO PLAN!

It is beyond the purpose of this volume to give detailed help on budget making because such is readily available in other literature. There are also a number of budgeting programs, such as Quicken, that are available online. Other resources can be found at the end of this book.

My objective here is to challenge you to rethink your present financial plan (budget). Could there be a better way to utilize the resources you have? As a steward, it is your responsibility to find out. Why should you continue doing things the same way year after year, when a little time and thought could generate improvement? If anyone should feel motivated to make the most of financial resources, it is the Christian. As a believer, you are under divine orders, and all that you possess has been entrusted to you by God, to whom you must give an account (Matthew 25:14–30). Improved financial planning is not only for your benefit but also for that of the kingdom of God (Matthew 6:33).

In rethinking your financial plan, let me suggest some further implications of Scripture. First things should always be first, and for the Christian the kingdom of God should be first. The promise of Matthew 6:33 is practical. We tend to get our priorities out of line. We place food, clothing, shelter, and pleasure first, and if anything is left over, we give an offering to the church. How contrary to the biblical pattern. It was the "firstfruits" that were to be given by Israel to the Lord, not the leftovers. Solomon was never more on target than when he said: "Honor the Lord with your wealth and with the best part of everything you produce. Then he will fill your barns with grain, and your vats will overflow with good wine" (Proverbs 3:9–10). Ever wonder why the barn is empty? Could it be that you have concentrated on the barn instead of the kingdom of God?

I would suggest that, from the very beginning of marriage, you set your budget to allocate the first 10 percent of your income for a thank offering to the Lord. After all, civil government insists that income tax be taken out even before you receive your check. Jesus was not opposed to such taxation but insisted that we should also "Give to God what belongs to God" (Matthew 22:17–22). On occasion, you will wish to give offerings beyond the tithe, but the tithe should be considered a minimal standard of giving for those couples who take biblical principles seriously.

PLAN TO SAVE!

Another implication for biblical budget-making is to plan for the future. "A prudent person foresees danger and takes precautions. The simpleton goes blindly on and suffers the consequences" (Proverbs 22:3). Throughout the Scriptures, the wise man or woman is the one who plans ahead to meet the needs of his or her family, business, or other endeavor (Luke 14:28–30). Planning ahead financially involves savings and investments. Unexpected difficulties will arise. You can count on it. Therefore, the wise steward plans ahead by saving. To fail to save a part of one's income is poor planning.

Together you should agree on the percentage that you would like to save, but something should be saved on a regular basis. Many Christian financial advisors suggest that 10 percent be allotted to savings and investments. You may choose more or less, but the choice is yours. If you save what is left after other matters are cared for, you will not save. Why not make yourself your "number-one creditor"? After tithing, pay yourself before you pay anyone else.

The couple who saves a percentage of their income regularly will have not only the reserve funds they need for emergencies but will also have the satisfied feeling that comes from being good stewards. Contrary to what some Christians seem to think, one is not more spiritual because he spends all that he makes. (According to some, this is supposed to exercise more faith in God to provide for emergency needs. In my opinion, it is simply a sign of poor stewardship.) Regular savings ought to be a part of your financial plan.

If you give 10 percent to the Lord's work and save 10 percent, that leaves 80 percent to be divided among mortgage payments (or rent), heat, electricity, telephone, water, insurance, furniture, food, medicines, clothes, transportation, education, recreation, Internet, newspapers, magazines, books, gifts, and so on. How this is distributed is your decision, but remember that you are a steward. You must give an account to God for 100 percent of your resources. The steward cannot afford the luxury of spending without thought. What is the best use of the 80 percent?

Quality does vary, and prices differ even for the same quality. Wise shopping does make a difference. In spite of the jokes we hear about the husband who spends five dollars on gas driving to the big-box store where he saves two dollars, the wise shopper can realize substantial savings. Such shopping takes time and energy. It is work and involves a great deal of insight, but the benefit will be revealed in extra money that may be applied to other needs or wants.

My wife and I have a standard procedure when she comes home from a shopping spree. I never ask how much she spent but how much she saved. It is more pleasant that way. Mastering the art of good shopping—including smart online shopping—is worth the effort involved.

Before I leave the subject of planning your expenditures, I suggest that you include in your plans some money for each partner to use as he or she wishes without accountability for every penny. This does not have to be a large amount, but a husband needs to be able to buy a candy bar without having to ask his wife for a dollar.

BUY NOW . . . PAY MUCH MORE LATER

Another extremely important matter that needs to be discussed by every couple is credit buying. If I had a red flag, I would wave it here. The media scream from every corner, "Buy now, pay later." What is not stated is that if you buy now without cash, you will pay much more later. Interest rates on charge accounts have a wide range. Some are 11, 12, or 15 percent, but many are 18 or 21 percent, or even higher. Couples need to read the small print. Credit is a privilege for which you must pay, and the cost is not the same on all plans.

Credit cards are a way of life in contemporary society. If used responsibly, they can help us keep records, and provide a good credit rating, which will be helpful when we apply for a mortgage loan. However, for many couples the credit card has led to membership in "The Society of the Financially Frustrated." The card encourages impulse buying, and most of us have more impulses than we can afford to follow. The responsible couple will use the credit card only for purchases they can afford to buy. They will not yield to the lure of "buy now, pay much more later." Why do we use credit? Because we want now what we cannot pay for now. In the purchase of a house, that may be a wise financial move. We would have to pay rent anyway. If the house is well selected, it will appreciate in value. If we have money for the down payment and can afford the monthly payments, such a purchase is wise. On the other hand, most of our purchases do not appreciate in value. Their value begins to decrease the day we buy them. We buy them before we can afford them. We pay the purchase price plus the interest charges for credit, while the article itself continues to depreciate in value. Why? For the momentary pleasure that the item brings. I simply ask, Is this the sign of responsible stewardship?

I know that there are certain "necessities" in our society, but why should a young married couple think they must obtain in the first year of marriage what it took their parents thirty years to accumulate? Why must you have the biggest and best now? With such a philosophy you destroy the joy of aspiration and attainment. You attain immediately. The joy is short-lived, and then you spend months in pain while you try to pay for it. Why saddle yourself with such unnecessary pressure?

The "necessities" of life are relatively few. I am not opposed to aspiring for more and better "things," if these can be used for good, but I am suggesting that you live in the present rather than in the future. Leave future joys for future accomplishments. Enjoy today what you have today.

For many years, my wife and I have played a little game that we have come to enjoy very much. It is called "Let's see how many things we can do without that everyone else thinks they must have." It all started in graduate school days out of necessity, but we got "hooked" and have continued to play it.

The Christian couple who will channel this creativity toward financial needs will find significant assets.

The game works like this. On Friday night or Saturday you go together to, say, Target, and walk down the aisles, looking at whatever catches your eye. Read labels, talk about how fascinating each item is, and then turn to each other and say, "Isn't it great that we don't have to have that!" Then while others walk out with arms loaded, names duly signed, you walk out hand in hand, excited that you do not need "things" to be happy. I highly recommend this game to all young married couples.

Let me clarify. I am not suggesting that you never buy anything on credit. I am suggesting that such credit purchases ought to be preceded by prayer, discussion, and, if needed, advice from a trusted financial counselor. If these steps had been taken, many Christian couples who are today imprisoned in financial bondage would be walking our streets as free men and women. I do not believe that it is God's will for His children to be in bondage. Many in our day are in such bondage because of unwise credit purchases.

STRETCH YOUR BUDGET BY BEING CREATIVE

Another practical implication of biblical truth with regard to financial matters has to do with our creative ability. Humans are instinctively creative. The museums of art and industry located across our world bear silent but visual witness to this creativity. We are made in the image of a God who creates, and we who bear His image have tremendous creative potential. The Christian couple who will channel this creativity toward financial needs will find significant assets. Creative crafts, sewing, refinishing used furniture, recycling others' discards, and so on can do wonders for the budget. Using special creative abilities may also lead you to the production of marketable items that may bring additional income, and there are many online sites where these can be sold.

Some years ago, I took a few college students to Chiapas, the southernmost state of Mexico, for a visit to Wycliffe Bible Translators' Jungle Camp. Here we observed missionaries being trained in the technique of living in tropical environments. They learned how to build houses, ovens, chairs, beds, all out of materials available in the jungle. I have reflected upon that experience many times. If that same creativity could be used by the average Christian couple in America, what could be accomplished? I am not suggesting that you build your own house; I am suggesting that you use your creativity for good—your own and others'.

THE MONEY TEAM

Now comes the question "Who will keep the books?" I believe that the couple should decide definitely who will pay bills and do the banking online, track any investments, and see that the funds are spent according to the plan upon which you have agreed. It may be the husband or the wife. Since you are a team, why not use the one best qualified for the task? As a couple discusses financial details, it will usually be obvious which one is more adept at such matters. One newlywed couple of our acquaintance began their marriage with the husband keeping the books, but quickly realized that the wife was much more adept at such things—and the husband was relieved to turn over the responsibility!

This does not mean that the one chosen to keep the books is in charge of making financial decisions. Such decisions are to be made as a team. The bookkeeper may not necessarily remain bookkeeper forever. For one reason or another you may agree after the first six months that it would be far wiser if the other partner became the bookkeeper. It is your marriage, and you are responsible for making the most of your resources.

Be certain, however, that the one who is not keeping the books knows how to do so and has full knowledge regarding various checking and savings accounts and investments. This is wise stewardship in view of the fact that one of you will likely die before the other. Christian stewardship demands that you be realistic.

IN CLOSING

If you remember that you are a team and therefore work as a team—following the biblical guidelines discussed in this chapter, seeking practical help where needed, and agreeing upon financial decisions—you will find money to be your faithful servant. If, however, you disregard the biblical principles and "do what comes naturally," you will soon find yourself in the same financial crisis that has become a way of life to thousands of Christian couples. If you are currently feeling the pain of crisis, it is time for a radical change—today. There is a way out. If you cannot think clearly enough to solve the problem, then by all means seek the counsel of your local banker or a Christian friend who is adept in financial matters. Do not continue to allow finances to cripple your walk with God—but use them as a means to an end, to serve and enhance your life with Him.

Being a unified money team does not guarantee you will have the marriage you always wanted, of course. However, it's an important element of a healthy marriage. After all, oneness and unity—with God and each other—mark a marriage of purpose and fulfillment. Find such unity in communication, decision making, sexual expression, finances, and the daily duties in your relationship, and you may soon find you are living the marriage you always wanted.

Your Turn

1. *Evaluate your financial status. For one month keep detailed records of how you spend your money. At the end of the month, list categories and amount spent for each item. Add to this list the monthly portion of any semiannual or annual payments that you may have, such as auto insurance. This will give you a realistic picture of your expenditures compared with your income (allow for incidentals).*

2. *Do you give at least 10 percent of your income to the Lord's work? Do you agree that you should?*

3. *Do you place at least 10 percent of your income into some savings or investment plan? Do you agree that you should?*

4. *Draw up a monthly plan that would give the first 10 percent of your income to the Lord, the second 10 percent to yourself (savings), and divide the remaining 80 percent among your other expenses. (If you are deeply in debt, this might require extending some of your debts or making a new loan with the bank to cover all existing debts so as to arrange smaller monthly payments.)*

5. *Discuss the above with your mate and seek agreement to follow such a plan. If you cannot work out such a plan alone, consult a Christian financial planner for assistance.*

6. *Discuss with your mate the role of credit cards in your financial plan. Seek to come to some agreement as to their function.*

7. *Can you agree that neither of you will ever again make a major purchase without consulting the partner? Agree upon the dollar value of a "major purchase" (for example, fifty dollars).*

8. *Do you feel financially free? If not, what will you do to change your situation? Discuss it with your mate and take action immediately.*

EPILOGUE

I'VE NEVER MET A couple who married with the intention of making each other miserable. Most people want to have a loving, supportive, understanding spouse. I'm convinced the fastest way to have such a spouse is to become a loving, supportive, understanding spouse.

If your spouse will read these chapters with you and complete and discuss with you the assignments, I believe you will find yourselves discovering the marriage you've always wanted. If your spouse is unwilling, then I hope you still will apply these concepts to your own life. Work on developing a positive attitude, expressed in loving words and actions. As you allow God to work in your heart, you can become an instrument of positive influence on your spouse.

Marital growth requires time and effort, but it begins by taking the first step. I hope that this book will help you take that step. If you find the book helpful, I hope you will share it with your friends who also have dreams of a happy marriage. Though I don't have time to respond personally to every inquiry, I'd be happy to hear of your progress toward the marriage you've always wanted, at www.garychapman.org.

NOTES

INTRODUCTION

1. The Barna Group, "Born Again Christians Just as Likely to Divorce as Are Non-Christians," September 8, 2004, *The Barna Update*, http://www.barna.org.

CHAPTER 4: "LISTEN TO ME!"

1. James Dobson, *The New Hide and Seek* (Grand Rapids: Revell, 1999), 195.
2. Ibid., 17–53.
3. Ibid., 196.

CHAPTER 7: "YOU MEAN WE HAVE TO WORK AT SEX?"

1. Lawrence K. Altman, "Study Finds That Teenage Virginity Pledges Are Rarely Kept," *New York Times,* March 10, 2004, A20; as cited in Ronald J. Sider, "The Scandal of the Evangelical Conscience," *Books and Culture,* January/February 2005, 39; http://www. christianitytoday.com/bc/2005/janfeb/3.8.html.
2. See William G. Axinn and Arland Thorton, "The Relationship between Cohabitation and Divorce: Selectivity or Casual Influence?" *Demography* 29 (1992): 357–74; and Zheng Wu, "Premarital Cohabitation and Postmarital Cohabiting Union Formation," *Journal of Family Issues* 16 (1995): 212–32.

RESOURCES

COMMUNICATION/GROWING CLOSER

BOOKS

Carder, Dave. *Close Calls: What Adulterers Want You to Know about Protecting Your Marriage*. Chicago: Moody, 2008. Protect your marriage by recognizing pitfalls before they trap you. Discover issues about your family of origin, know your dangerous partner profile, identify when you might be vulnerable for infidelity.

Chapman, Gary. *Desperate Marriages: Moving toward Hope and Healing in Your Relationship*. Chicago: Northfield, 2008. If you're in a troubled marriage, don't give up. You can learn to recognize what is holding you back, take responsibility for your own thoughts and actions, and make choices that have a lasting impact on you and your spouse.

———. *Happily Ever After*. Carol Stream, IL: Tyndale, 2011. Every couple has disagreements. All too often, though, when we engage in arguments, our goal is not to resolve the conflict at hand but rather to win the fight. Good marriages are based on friendship, not on winning arguments. Gary Chapman provides couples with a simple blueprint for achieving win-win solutions to everyday conflicts.

———. *The 5 Love Languages: The Secret to Love That Lasts*. Chicago: Northfield, 1995, 2004, 2010. Dr. Chapman's signature book on how to show love by using the love language that is most meaningful to your spouse: words of affirmation, gifts, acts of service, quality time, physical touch.

———. *The Four Seasons of Marriage*. Carol Stream, IL: Tyndale, 2007. Marriages are perpetually in a state of transition, continually moving from one season to another. Each season holds the potential for emotional health, happiness, and challenges. This book describes the recurring seasons of marriage, helps you identify your season, and shows you how to enhance your marriage in all seasons.

————. *Now You're Speaking My Language*. Nashville: B&H, 2007. When you offer loyalty, forgiveness, empathy, and commitment to resolving conflict, you'll not only have a happier marriage, but you'll encourage each other in spiritual growth.

Chapman, Gary, and Jennifer Thomas. *When Sorry Isn't Enough: Making Things Right with Those You Love*. Chicago: Northfield, 2013. Sometimes, saying "I'm sorry" just doesn't cut it. This groundbreaking study of the way we apologize reveals that it's not a matter of will—it's a matter of how. By helping you identify the languages of apology, this book clears the way toward healing and sustaining your relationships.

Eggerichs, Emerson. *Love and Respect: The Love She Most Desires; The Respect He Desperately Needs*. Nashville: Thomas Nelson, 2004. It's simple: a wife needs to feel loved and a husband needs to feel respected. This bestseller explains and offers practical ways to show love and respect.

Feldhahn, Shaunti. *For Women Only: What You Need to Know about the Inner Lives of Men*. Sisters, OR: Multnomah, 2004, 2013. Guidance for women who want to understand their husbands and provide the loving support that modern men need and want.

Feldhahn, Shaunti, and Jeff Feldhahn. *For Men Only: A Straightforward Guide to the Inner Lives of Women*. Sisters, OR: Multnomah, 2006, 2013. Are women really that complicated and impossible to understand? This book shows that women are actually easy to please once you understand what they need.

Harley Jr., Willard. *His Needs, Her Needs: Building an Affair-Proof Marriage*. Grand Rapids: Revell, 2001, 2011. In this bestseller, marriage counselor Willard Harley identifies the ten most vital needs for husbands and wives and shows them how to satisfy these needs in their marriage. He follows this volume with *His Needs, Her Needs for Parents: Keeping Romance Alive* (Revell, 2003).

Keller, Timothy. *The Meaning of Marriage: Facing the Complexities of Commitment with the Wisdom of God*. New York: Dutton, 2011. Aiming to write a book on marriage that will be relevant to just about anyone of any age and stage in life, the author, with helpful insight from his wife, seeks to tackle some of the common misconceptions and mysteries of marriage while providing biblically based instruction on what a great marriage looks like.

Kendrick, Alex and Stephen Kendrick. *The Love Dare*. Nashville: B&H, 2008, 2013. Featured in the popular film *Fireproof*, *The Love Dare* is a forty-day devotional including a Scripture, principle, and daily "dare." When a husband or wife begins to think "I don't love you anymore," it may be that he or she does not understand true love. *The Love Dare* will lead you back to loving your mate while learning what true love really is. Also check out the *Fireproof Your Marriage Couple's Kit* by Jennifer Dion (Outreach, Inc., 2008).

Parker Jr., Johnny C. *Renovating Your Marriage Room by Room*. Chicago: Moody, 2012. After the honeymoon is over, most couples find marriage to not be what they expected. Using the ultimate tool, the Word of God, Dr. Parker will walk you through each room of your marriage, and encourage you to get to work on the rebuilding.

Thomas, Gary. *Sacred Marriage*. Grand Rapids: Zondervan, 2000. God's primary intent for your marriage is not to make you happy, it's to make you holy. The author looks at how God uses marriage to teach us respect, develop our prayer life, reveal our sins, build perseverance, develop a forgiving spirit, and much more.

WEBSITES

FamilyLife.com: Articles and practical help on improving a healthy marriage, healing a troubled one, romance and sex, spiritual growth, even holidays and special occasions.

5LoveLanguages.com: Advice and resources on relationship issues from world-renowned author, speaker, and counselor Dr. Gary Chapman. Also features the 30-second assessment tool for determining your love language.

FocusontheFamily.com: An abundance of resources on many areas and issues pertaining to marriage and family life.

MarriagePartnership.com: This site contains numerous practical articles with a biblical viewpoint on marriage-related issues.

2Becoming1.com: Many resources available, including the *Two Becoming One* book and workbook by marriage experts Don and Sally Meredith. Learn to integrate the practical and spiritual sides of marriage.

MoneyandMarriage.org: This site is loaded with resources on the important connection between finances and marriage.

FINANCES

BOOKS

Blue, Ron with Jeremy White. *The New Master Your Money: A Step-by-Step Plan for Gaining and Enjoying Financial Freedom*. Chicago: Moody, 2004; also, *The New Master Your Money Workbook: A Ten-Week Program*. If you worry about money, dip into savings to pay bills, or find yourself unable to stick to a budget, this book offers hope. Identify and create both short and long-term financial goals with this practical resource.

Dayton, Howard. *Free and Clear: God's Road Map to Debt-Free Living*. Chicago: Moody, 2006. Though debt has become a way of life for millions, it causes stress and complicates marriages. Learn biblical money management practices that will restore your financial health and refresh your spirit. Yes, it is possible to be free and clear!

———. *Money and Marriage God's Way*. Chicago: Moody, 2009. Money is an important part of life and too often the source of stress for couples. Learn the basics of both marriage and finances and how you can become closer as you work together in this area.

—————. *Your Money Map: A 7-Step Guide to True Financial Freedom.* Chicago: Moody, 2006. Realistic steps and the necessary tools to follow the seven destinations on the money map, offering principles that work wherever you are financially.

Jenkins, Lee. *Lee Jenkins on Money: Real Solutions to Financial Challenges.* Chicago: Moody, 2009. Drawing from questions he is asked as he presents financial seminars, expert Lee Jenkins answers the everyday money questions most couples have. A valuable reference to keep handy.

Kay, Ellie. *Half-Price Living: Secrets to Living Well on One Income.* Chicago: Moody, 2007. If you're faced with living on one income through desire or necessity, this book written by America's Family Financial Expert™ gives you plenty of ideas on living on less and making a home-based business work within your family life.

Kay, Ellie. *A Tip a Day with Ellie Kay: 12 Months' Worth of Money-Saving Ideas.* Moody, 2008. Practical, creative tips on saving money on everything from groceries and clothing to life insurance and vacations.

Ramsey, Dave. *The Money Answer Book: Quick Answers to Everyday Financial Questions.* Nashville: Thomas Nelson, 2005. Popular financial expert Dave Ramsey answers your questions.

WEBSITES

Crown.org: Resources for every area of financial management including debt reduction, investment, biblical principles regarding money, and information about local Crown financial coaches.

DaveRamsey.com: Offers many resources as well as information on Financial Peace University classes, which explain Dave Ramsey's methods for paying off all debt and provide knowledge and tools to change your financial behavior and relieve the stress that surrounds money issues.

GoodSenseMinistry.com: Willow Creek Association's information for individuals and material suitable for training/teaching church groups about biblical financial principles.

KingdomAdvisors.org: A site to help you find a financial advisor who will counsel you from a biblical perspective.

Mint.com: A basic, free online budget tracker that will help you to see where every dollar is going. Mint also has a mobile app to make budgeting more convenient and accessible.

MoneyandMarriage.org: Many resources pertaining to the important link between financial and marital health, debt-reduction, and much more. Also available on this site: the Money Map Personality I.D. profile.

Quicken.com: Quicken is a practical, easy-to-use budgeting software that connects with your bank(s), sorts your expenses into categories, and sets up a realistic budget according to one's income, debt, and spending history.

SEXUAL INTIMACY

Chapman, Gary. *Happily Ever After*. Carol Stream, IL: Tyndale, 2011. Is there a difference between "Let's have sex" and "Let's make love"? You bet! Sex is the joining of bodies, but love is the joining of souls. Sex without love will never be ultimately satisfying, but sex that grows out of love will take a marriage to a whole new level of satisfaction. Learn how to first love and then experience greater sexual satisfaction.

Leman, Kevin. *Turn Up the Heat: A Couples Guide to Sexual Intimacy*. Grand Rapids: Revell, 2009. Even married people have questions about sex, but don't always know who to ask. In this volume, the author of *Sheet Music* answers common questions about sex and intimacy.

Rosberg, Gary, and Barbara Rosberg. *The 5 Sex Needs of Men and Women*. Carol Stream, IL: Tyndale, 2007. The Rosbergs explain the five deepest sexual needs of both men and women, how to meet your spouse's needs, and why the Golden Rule needs to be reinterpreted when it comes to sex. They discuss problems caused by unmet needs and how to meet those needs.

Wheat, Ed, and Gaye Wheat. *Intended for Pleasure: Sexual Technique and Sexual Fulfillment in Christian Marriage*, 3rd ed. Grand Rapids: Revell, 1997. The classic on sex in Christian marriage is an easy-to-read reference book that gently encourages the married couple to make their sexual relationship the fulfilling experience it was meant to be. This is a complete sex manual for practicing Christians with basic facts, illustrations, and candid discussion of all facets of human sexuality.

DEVOTIONAL

There are many fine devotional materials for individuals, couples, and families. These are just a sampling:

Chapman, Gary and Ramon Presson. *101 Conversation Starters for Couples* and *101 Conversation Starters for Families*. Chicago: Northfield, 2002.

Chapman, Gary. *The Love Languages Devotional Bible*. Chicago: Moody, 2012. This devotional Bible takes Dr. Gary Chapman's groundbreaking love languages concepts and puts them into a daily devotional format that helps you apply them to your life every day.

Dobson, James, and Shirley Dobson. *Night Light: A Devotional for Couples*. Carol Stream, IL: Tyndale, 2008.

Rosberg, Gary, and Barbara Rosberg. *Renewing Your Love: Devotions for Couples*. Carol Stream, IL: Tyndale, 2003.

Sartor, Toni, and Pamela McQuade. *365 Daily Devotions for Couples: Inspiration for the Marriage You've Always Wanted*. Grand Rapids: Barbour, 2007.